THE BLESSING OF ABRAHAM

Christopher Wickland

DEDICATION

I dedicate this book to all who have a love for Israel and God's word.

I want to thank...

Jesus,

My Wife for her tireless patience with me

and all who have helped me on the journey.

Also a very special thank you to Sandra Goodman and Sally Marston who worked hard on editing and proof reading this manuscript. I am in your debt.

Also thank you to all who encourage me to keep on keeping on.

THE BLESSING OF ABRAHAM

Written by
Reverend Christopher Wickland

Unless otherwise stated, Scriptures are taken from:

New International Version, Copyright 1973, 1978, 1984 by the international Bible Society.

New Living Translation, Copyright 1996, 2004, 2007 by Tyndale House Foundation. Used by permission of Tyndale House Publishers, Inc., Carol Stream, Illinois 60188. All rights reserved.

ESV Bible (English Standard Version), copyright 2011 by Crossway, a publishing ministry of Good News Publishers. Used by permission, all rights reserved.

NASB (New American Standard Bible) copyright 1960, 1962, 1963, 1968, 1971, 1972, 1973, 1975, 1977, 1995 by the Lockman foundation. Used by permission. www.Lockman.org

Complete Jewish Bible copyright 1998 and 2016 by David H. Stern. Used by permission. All rights reserved worldwide.

Holman Christian Standard Bible®
Copyright © 1999, 2000, 2002, 2003, 2009 by Holman Bible Publishers. Used with permission by Holman Bible Publishers, Nashville, Tennessee. All rights reserved.

All rights reserved. This book or any portion thereof may not be reproduced or used in any manner whatsoever without the express written permission of the publisher except for the use of brief quotations in a book review or scholarly journal.

All *Italics*, underlining and **bold** font on any scripture, has been done so by the author for emphasis.

Copyright © 2018 by Christopher Wickland

CONTENTS

Page 11	Introduction	
Page 13	Chapter 1	(The Blessing)
Page 17	Chapter 2	(Sowing and Reaping)
Page 19	Chapter 3	(The Tree of Death)
Page 22	Chapter 4	(The Fall Part 1)
Page 26	Chapter 5	(The Fall Part 2)
Page 29	Chapter 6	(The New Creation)
Page 33	Chapter 7	(Expulsion From The Blessing)
Page 40	Chapter 8	(Blessing Revoked)
Page 44	Chapter 9	(Offerings To God)
Page 48	Chapter 10	(The Hidden Code of Salvation)
Page 50	Chapter 11	(Seed Time and Harvest)
Page 52	Chapter 12	(God Blesses Noah)
Page 54	Chapter 13	(The Call of Abram)
Page 56	Chapter 14	(The Blessing of Abraham Prt 1)
Page 58	Chapter 15	(The Blessing of Abraham Prt 2)
Page 61	Chapter 16	(Abraham was Rich)
Page 65	Chapter 17	(The Blessing of Abraham Prt 3)
Page 67	Chapter 18	(The Blessing of Abraham Prt 4)
Page 71	Chapter 19	(Abram meets Melchizedek)
Page 77	Chapter 20	(The Tithe)
Page 83	Chapter 21	(Time for a New Name)
Page 89	Chapter 22	(The Multiplication Principle)
Page 94	Chapter 23	(Blessing During Famine)
Page 100	Chapter 24	(The Blessing Continued)
Page 106	Conclusions	

INTRODUCTION

PLEASE READ ME!

When you start to read a book, you may be the kind of person, like me, who skips the introduction to get straight down to business. Well, this is an introduction not to be missed!

A couple of years ago, I felt the Holy Spirit impress upon me, the need to study 'The blessing of Abraham.' At the time I didn't really see its relevance, so 'held off' until a year or so later. Then I was shocked at what I uncovered. In fact, in all honesty, I couldn't believe that what I was studying could possibly be true. Yet, the deeper I delved, the more acute the thought became - was I wrong in my understanding of the Gospel? I soon realised that the Abrahamic Blessing was not just for the Jew, but also for the Gentile, through Jesus Christ. I also realised, that I had been preaching a diminished, sanitised and 'safe' Gospel, one which proclaimed a 'salvation only' message. In fact, my understanding of the Gospel was so narrow in its application, that I had blinded myself to its wondrous glory, mystery and power.

There will be some chapters in this book that may be challenging to believe and difficult to get your head around. Sadly, our church cultures and religiosities have robbed us of more than we could know. The apostle Paul states in Romans, "the Gospel is the power of God to salvation." Yet it is a power which too few of us have seen and experienced. Why is this? Because, I would say, we haven't really understood exactly what 'the Gospel' is.

So, this book has been written to address this and help Christians understand just how deep, wide and glorious the Gospel really is. A book which is devoted to the unpacking of one single verse in the New Testament, found in the book of Galatians, chapter 3:13-14 *'Christ redeemed us from the curse of the law by becoming a curse for us—for it is written, "Cursed is everyone who is hanged on a tree"—**so that in Christ Jesus*** *the blessing of Abraham might come to the Gentiles, so that we might receive the promised Spirit through faith.'* ESV

This verse essentially contains the core element of the Gospel. But like most of the apostle Paul's writings, each verse alone contains volumes of revelation and knowledge. So, to unpack Galatians 3:13-14, we must go right back to the beginning of the bible, where we started from, how we fell into spiritual bondage and death and came under the curse. Once this foundation is laid, we will then better understand why God wants to bring us back into The Blessing.

What is 'The Blessing', you may be asking, and many I am sure would struggle to give an appropriate answer. Some Christians would even try to talk themselves out of being blessed by God. Why? In my opinion it could be misplaced humility, a wrong understanding of God and possibly the fear of being painted with the 'prosperity gospel' brush. The truth is, God is a loving heavenly Father and He wants to bless us!

As there always needs to be balance and tension in the Christian walk, we need to be aware that the Kingdom of God is upon the earth now, but not yet in all its fullness, which will only come when Jesus returns. Theologians call this 'Kingdom now, but not yet.', meaning, we can still see, expect and experience incredible aspects of God's Kingdom upon the earth, right here, right now.

I trust this book will help to expand your understanding of the Gospel and reveal the power and nature of the Abrahamic Blessing. When you realise you are blessed to be a blessing, then the sky is the limit! A whole new world is awaiting you, but first, you need the keys, the understanding and the biblical foundation to walk it out in confident faith.

CHAPTER ONE

THE BLESSING

Genesis 1:28-30 *'And **God blessed them**, and God said unto them, be fruitful, and multiply, and replenish the earth, and subdue it: and **have dominion** over the fish of the sea, and over the fowl of the air, and over every living thing that moves upon the earth. And God said, behold, I have given you every herb bearing seed, which is upon the face of the earth, and every tree, in the which is the fruit of a tree yielding seed; for you it shall be for food. And to every beast of the earth, and to every fowl of the air, and to everything that creeps upon the earth, wherein there is life, I have given every green herb for meat; and it was so.'* KJV

We begin with a glimpse of the wonderful relationship Adam and Eve had with God in the Garden of Eden - a place of great blessing. In this passage we see a lovely picture of them given in marriage. God, who is an exuberant Father, is so happy and overjoyed with His beautiful creation, He just wants to bless His newly-weds with wonderful gifts from His goodness and treasures. Sometimes when we read the bible, we can be guilty of seeing God as cold, matter of fact and distant. But it is knowing the heart of Jesus, which is the heart of the Father, that reveals to us Who He really is - a passionate God, not devoid of emotion. He is intensely interested in the affairs of His children because He is our King, our Father, our Friend, our Brother and our Saviour. Our God is a good God!

Having released His blessing upon Adam and Eve, God then spoke over them a command to be fruitful and multiply. When we read this passage we generally only think of one thing, having loads and loads of children! This is very likely the primary context of the passage. Yet, as God chooses His words very carefully for they are Spirit and Truth, it is also God's will for Adam and Eve to be fruitful in every respect. As we can see from the following New Testament scriptures, God still wants us to be a fruitful people:

Colossians 1:9-10 *'And so, from the day we heard, we have not ceased to pray for you, asking that you may be filled with the knowledge of his will in all spiritual wisdom and understanding, so as to walk in a manner worthy of the Lord, fully pleasing to him: **bearing fruit** in every good work and increasing in the knowledge of God;'* ESV

3 John 2 *'Beloved, I pray that in all respects you may prosper and be in good health, just as your soul prospers.'* NASB

Galatians 5:22-23 *'But the **fruit** of the Spirit is love, joy, peace, patience, kindness, goodness, faithfulness, gentleness, self-control; against such things there is no law.'* ESV

John 15:5 *'I am the vine; you are the branches. Whoever abides in me and I in him, he it is that bears **much fruit**, for apart from me you can do nothing.'* ESV

To be a fruitful believer is part of God's blessing over our lives. He has blessed us with EVERY SPIRITUAL BLESSING in Christ (Ephesians 1:3). In other words, there is nothing spiritually left for God to bless us with! But do not over spiritualise this truth by thinking that the Old Testament is purely physical blessing and the New Testament, spiritual. Of course, being born again and a new creation in Christ Jesus is spiritual, but when Jesus went to the cross, He didn't just die for your spirit, He died to save the whole man; spirit, soul and body. Your spirit IS saved, your soul is BEING saved and your flesh WILL be saved on the last day.

1 Thessalonians 5:23 *'Now may the God of peace Himself sanctify you entirely; and may your **spirit and soul and body** be preserved complete, without blame at the coming of our Lord Jesus Christ.'* NASB

So, back to Genesis 1:28. We have looked at the command to be fruitful, but God also wanted them to multiply, fill the earth, subdue it and have dominion over it. In a later chapter we will see this multiplication at work in the Jewish nation, which ultimately led to the birth of Messiah. Today, God's word is still multiplying by bringing many Gentiles into the blessing of Abraham. This blessing of multiplication is not to be taken lightly! It is a key component of the blessing which God pours out on His people.

We can see the effect of the blessing to multiply, in various different ways throughout scripture. The account of the feeding the 5000 (Matthew 14:13-21) and the feeding of the 4000 (Matthew 15:29-39)
are examples of the blessing of miraculous multiplication. Also, we see the church in Acts exploding in growth from 120 people in an upper room to 3000 in one day. The word of God itself multiplies by spreading and flourishing as we see in the following scriptures:

Acts 12:24 *'But the word of God **increased and multiplied**.'* ESV

Acts 6:7 *'And the word of God continued to **increase**, and the number of the disciples **multiplied** greatly in Jerusalem, and a great many of the priests became obedient to the faith.'* ESV

Acts 19:20 *'So the word of the Lord continued to **increase** and prevail mightily.'* ESV

You may be thinking that the blessing spoken of in Genesis 1:28 is only for Adam and Eve before the fall, and yes, you would be correct. However, we will later see that this blessing, placed on Abraham, is for **all** his seed. That includes the believing Gentiles, which means you and me! So, we can say for sure that the principles we are learning from Genesis 1:28 are very applicable to us as New Testament believers. God wants to bless you, He wants you to be fruitful, He wants you to increase and multiply, He wants you to have dominion and grow in exercising the authority He has given you through Christ Jesus.

So, Adam and Eve, indeed mankind as a whole, had started from a place of great blessing. The fall of man brought in the curse which still to this day dominates mankind. However, God's heart is to bless but the only way to restore the blessing and intimacy with God, would be via covenant.

CHAPTER TWO

SOWING AND REAPING

Genesis 1:29 *'And God said, Behold, I have given you every herb bearing seed, which is upon the face of the earth, and every tree, in which is the fruit of a tree yielding seed; to you it shall be for food.'* KJV

We see in this verse how God starts to teach mankind the principles of sowing and reaping. God gave to man 'every herb bearing seed', which has the ability to reproduce itself many times over. Also, we learn that the earth, and the first and second heavens operate under the same principle. Indeed, all truth is parallel! That which we can see in the natural, is true in the spiritual and thus effects the first (visible) heaven, the second heaven (where the demonic and angelic reside), as well as the third heaven (where God and His angels reside). The following scriptures make this clear:

Genesis 1:1 *'In the beginning, God created the __heavens__ (plural) and the earth.'* ESV (My parenthesis added)

Daniel 10:13 *'But for twenty-one days the spirit prince of the kingdom of Persia blocked my way. Then Michael, one of the archangels, came to help me, and I left him there with the spirit prince of the kingdom of Persia...'* NLT (Warfare in the heavenly realms)

Revelation 12:7-9 *'Now war arose in heaven, Michael and his angels fighting against the dragon. And the dragon and his angels fought back, but he was defeated, and there was no longer any place for them in heaven. And the great dragon was thrown down, that ancient serpent, who is called the devil and Satan, the deceiver of the whole world—he was thrown down to the earth, and his angels were thrown down with him.* Verse 12 *'Therefore, rejoice, __O heavens and you who dwell in them!__ But woe to you, O earth and sea, for the devil has come down to you in great wrath, because he knows that his time is short!"* ESV

2 Corinthians 12:2 *'I know a man in Christ who fourteen years ago was caught up to __the third heaven__—whether in the body or out of the body I do not know, God knows.'* ESV

Genesis 1:29 teaches us a wonderful parallel truth. Just as in the natural, seeds lead to fruitfulness and when harvested lead to more seeds to plant. Likewise, God provides His Word for us to 'sow' as seed into our lives, and then, in due season, it too will multiply and bear fruits of The Kingdom (Mark 4:14).

As a farmer lives his life in cycles of sowing and reaping, so we too should always be sowing and always reaping. When we begin to understand this principle, like the farmer, we will appreciate that there is a time gap between when we sow and when we reap. Once the believer is in a place of continuous sowing, they can expect to be always at some point, in a season of continual harvest. This is what I call the 'overflow'. This is where we are constantly sowing to the things of God's word and His Spirit, and in the course of time consistently reaping a harvest of fruitfulness.

The principle of sowing and reaping is a key revelation and a theme running throughout all of scripture. So, if we tend to think of sowing and reaping in a negative context, we should rather consider that it is a universal law of God that operates in both the natural world and the spiritual. Remember, you can make this work for you for good as well as bad, so understanding this principle will be key to turning your life around from lack, sickness and poverty of spirit; to great joy, peace and prosperity in the things of God and His Spirit.

CHAPTER THREE

THE TREE OF THE KNOWLEDGE OF GOOD AND EVIL AKA THE TREE OF DEATH!

Genesis 2:17 *'But of the tree of the knowledge of good and evil, you shall not eat of it, for in the day that you eat of it you will surely die.'* MEV

When Adam and Eve disobeyed God and ate fruit from the tree of the knowledge of good and evil, the consequence for them was immediate. Their spiritual covering, which had come from being divinely connected to God, was now lost, and so they became aware of their nakedness.

Notice how man tries to cover himself - fig leaves! The sad reality is that Adam and Eve were now all too aware of the flesh and their carnal nature. The covering they had enjoyed was so utterly complete that wearing clothes was never an issue! They had been living in the rest of God (Hebrews 4:1-3), just (justified), righteous and holy, but now they were in a place of guilt, shame and fear, trying to justify themselves in God's eyes. In short, they had moved from being God- conscious to self-conscious. This must have been an awful burden to bear for Adam and Eve, especially knowing that their disease of sin would be passed onto their children and thus to all humanity.

The account of the trees in the garden, teaches us that the commandments of God are true and just, so we need to dispel the notion that observing certain rules is a bad thing. For instance, when God says, 'Do not commit adultery' (Exodus 20:14), it is not because God is trying to be a kill joy. No! He is trying to protect people from their own selfish shortsightedness. He is trying to spare people the heartache and pain of the breakdown of family and trust. So, when God gave the commandment in the garden not to eat of the tree, He was actually making Adam and Eve aware of His very best for them. Remember, God's word and commands to us, are good and holy, and we would do well to pay heed to them! Why? Because in being a doer of the word there is life and peace.

The question that needs to be asked is: 'Why did God put the tree of the knowledge of good and evil in the garden in the first place?' Why would God put something so ruthlessly toxic and dangerous in a place of such glory and beauty? Well, this tree wasn't in the garden to just give Adam and Eve a choice to love God or rebel. No, I believe there was something far deeper going on. James 1:13 makes it clear that God does not tempt people to sin. We know that satan is the one who does the tempting. Nevertheless, as God knew the end from the beginning, He knew what was going to go wrong before He created the earth, yet He still chose to do it this way. Why?

Revelation 13:8
'And all that dwell upon the earth shall worship him, whose names are not written in the book of life of **the Lamb slain from the foundation of the world.*'* KJV

Jesus was the Lamb slain before the foundation of the world, before the earth was created, before time began. So, was the 'Lamb of God' one of Jesus' eternal names, or did it *become* a title at some stage in eternity past? We do not know, but I suspect it may have been an eternal name. Just this small paragraph reveals that there was a lot more going on in the garden than merely a toxic tree. God was revealing the out-working of His redemptive plan, in all His glorious wisdom, an eternal plan of divine counsel to destroy the works of the devil (1 John 3:8) and elevate man from humble beginnings of flesh to being in the image of the Last Adam, the heavenly man, Jesus Christ (1 Corinthians 15:49).

In the garden there was no death or sickness up to this point, physically and spiritually man was immortal, with no fear of death and hell. In fact, hell was made for the devil and his angels (Matthew 25:41), it was never supposed to be a place for man to go to. To the person who bows down to serve a false god, I would say, beware! Or you will end up going to the place where your 'god' resides. There is only One True God, and His Name is Jesus. Every other so-called god is demonic, and the future for all demons is in hell. All the followers of Jesus go to heaven to be with Him when they die. All people who worship false gods will go to where their god resides. Hell!

It is not God who wants to send anyone to such a terrible place. The truth is, the legal right to choose whom we serve and thus our future destiny is very much up to us. 2 Peter 3:9 is very clear, *"God is not willing that any should perish"*. God doesn't want anyone to go to hell! Remember, we reap what we sow.

The account of the eating of the forbidden fruit is key to understanding the nature of sin, sickness, disease and the curse. Before the fall we know that everything in the garden was good. Then when the forbidden fruit was eaten, the seed of death was sown, and it was so ravenous and infectious that everything was affected by its impact and sprawl. When Jesus died on the cross He paid the price to do away with all sin, sickness, disease and curse. Have you ever wondered why Jesus wore a crown of thorns? Well, this crown of thorns represents the curse of creation, and on the day Jesus returns He will restore creation to its former glory, and release it fully from the curse (Romans 8:2, 8:19, Galatians 3:13).

CHAPTER 4

THE FALL Part 1

We now come to Genesis Chapter 3, where we have the story of the fall of mankind. Why is it called the fall? Good question! We know that Adam and Eve were made in the image of God, living in a state of perfection. As mentioned in the previous chapter, as soon as they had sinned, they lost God's covering and 'fell' from being in the image of God to being in the image of man (see Genesis 5:3). They 'fell' from being whole and sinless to fractured and sinful, from being healthy to the place of death both spiritually and physically. They moved from a beautiful perfect relationship with God to hiding from His presence.

In Genesis 3:1-6 we see that satan was permitted to tempt Adam and Eve. God did not intervene when satan deceived Eve into eating the fruit of the tree of the knowledge of good and evil. These verses are key to understanding spiritual authority. Whoever we listen to determines who's in charge of our lives! At the very moment Eve took of the fruit, she went from being a doer of God's word to being a doer of satan's word. Satan is the father of lies. Everything that comes from his mouth is a lie because of his nature (John 8:44). In fact, all satan's words are invalid and inoperable, they are death, destruction and woe. The reality is that all words are powerful tools in the natural realm. God's words however, are living and active, they are truth and life to all who find them (See Matthew 12:36, Hebrews 4:12, Jeremiah 1:12).

Adam and Eve were initially under God's authority and were operating in His delegated authority (Genesis 1:28). However, the moment that Adam and Eve disobeyed God they immediately came under a new spiritual authority - away from God and His word, to the devil and his lies. At that moment, a change of governance took place over their lives - from the God of life, peace, joy and blessing to the devil of death, strife, hate and cursing.

Genesis 3:1 *'...has God said, you shall not eat of every tree of the garden?'* NASB

It is interesting to see in this verse, how satan immediately spins the word of God so that the prohibition is focused upon, rather than, the blessing. Satan wanted Eve to focus on the one thing she was not allowed to do, instead of taking joy in everything else. Satan is always trying to undermine the word of God, he uses the same old tricks time and time again, 'Did God really say?', 'are you sure this is really what He wants?' If he can get us to doubt the integrity of God's word then he has managed to bait us to go from listening to the God of truth to listening to the father of lies. Satan will always try to make you think that God is the one who lacks integrity.

A Christian who walks and lives by the word of God alone is very dangerous to satan. They expose him to the light of God's power and authority, and he utterly hates this. If he can get us out of the light and into the shifting shadows of darkness, then he can make us lose our authority over him. It is good to remember that the devil hates the Christian who walks in utter and complete authority over him. If you want to please God and keep the devil at bay, be a doer of God's word. Do not doubt His integrity and power, even when it seems like it is not working. You need to 'keep on keeping on' until you get the breakthrough!

Ephesians 6:13 *'Therefore, take up the full armour of God, so that you will be able to resist in the evil day, **and having done everything, to stand firm.**'* NASB

So, having done everything, continue to stand firm! Being consistent is the key. The English word 'patience', means to be consistent under pressure. This is such an important lesson in the realm of walking by faith. Patience and faith always go hand in hand, because the way and path of faith has to be married to consistency, especially when the going gets tough. This is what the bible calls the *'good fight of faith'* and I feel this is a truth we tend to forget. Faith is not always easy, sometimes you just have to fight through 'stuff' to get the victory. I think the quicker we get this 'fight' mentality into our thinking the more we will press on and the less we will quit and fail.

Genesis 3:4 *'And the serpent said to the woman, you shall surely not die.'*

In this verse, satan comes out with an all-out lie. He has already managed to engage Eve in a conversation and made her question and doubt God's word. It seems that satan has endeared himself to Eve in such a way that she trusts him! So. now she is listening to him, he comes out with the lie, *'you shall surely not die.'* This lie completely contradicts and contravenes God's word.

This is one of satan's tricks that he uses consistently on unsuspecting humanity. For example, the bible says *'By His stripes you were healed'* (1 Peter 2:24), yet often the devil 'tries it on' with us, especially when we are weak and low, and a thought comes 'I am not worthy to be healed, only certain people but not me'. This is just a blatant lie! Don't believe it! Take every thought captive and speak God's word (2 Corinthians 10:5). God's word is the truth! Never believe a lie, no matter how real or convincing it may appear. It is still a lie. God's word is truth and it is eternal. It will never fail!

Genesis 3:5 *"For God knows that when you eat from it your eyes will be opened, and you will be like God, knowing good and evil."* NIV

Now that satan has sold the lie to Eve that she will not die, he can push the goodies of sin and rebellion. This is always his tactic. He will tell us a lie, then follow it up with some 'candy' for our flesh to enjoy. He will cause our flesh to lust for something that exceeds the fear of the consequence of disobeying the commandment.

James 1:14-15 *'but each person is tempted when they are dragged away by their own evil desire and enticed. Then, after desire has conceived, it gives birth to sin; and sin, when it is full-grown, gives birth to death.'* NIV

Satan will always use the power of desire to cause man to sin. Look at Genesis 3:6 *'When the woman saw that the fruit of the tree was good for food and pleasing to the eye, and also desirable for gaining wisdom, she took some and ate it. She also gave some to her husband, who was with her, and he ate it.'* NIV

The snare is now set, the bait is ready to be eaten, then snap! Adam and Eve have now fallen for a lie that will cost them everything.

CHAPTER FIVE

THE FALL Part 2

Genesis 3:7 *'And the eyes of them both were opened, and they knew that they were naked and they sewed fig leaves together, and made themselves aprons.'* KJV

It is here that something really tragic happened. Adam and Eve went from being immortal to being mortal. Their eyes were opened and they went from the bliss of walking in God's love, grace and Spirit, to the condemnation of the law and the flesh. They went from being confident and unashamed in God to being embarrassed, fearful and ashamed. They went from being people of faith who trusted in God to people of fear. They went from being sinless to being sinful. And so, the downward spiral continued. At the moment they listened and obeyed the devil, they placed him and his word above that of God's. In a moment of simple disobedience, Adam and Eve had inadvertently slipped from God's rule and dominion to that of satan, and had handed over to him their God-given blessing and authority.

We get a hint of this in Luke chapter 4:5-6 *'And he (satan) led Him (Jesus) up and showed Him all the kingdoms of the world in a moment of time. And the devil said to Him, "I will give You all this domain and its glory;* **for it has been handed over to me**, *and I give it to whomever I wish.'*

Notice how satan says that the power had been handed over to him and he could give it to whoever he wanted. This is what happened in the garden, when he tricked Adam and Eve and gained the legal rights to this earth. Satan became the god of this earth (2 Corinthians 4:4) and the prince of the second heaven (Ephesians 2:2). From then on, mankind was no longer in the image of God. Now all humanity takes on the image of the first Adam. *'And Adam lived a hundred and thirty years and begot* **in his own likeness after his image...**' *Genesis 5: 3*

So, Adam, who was originally created a little lower than God, descends and falls from his elevated position in creation, so much so that according to Hebrews 2:7, man is now a little lower than the angels and consequently subject to demonic beings and powerless to resist in his fallen state.

Another horrific legal conclusion arises. As we saw in Chapter 3, each person will spend eternity with their god, either the One True God or the false god of this age. Remember at the point of death there are two future realities, heaven or hell. The destination is down to who we serve and live for. It is God's will that none should perish (2 Peter 3:8-10), but at the end of the day all humanity has a choice to make. The bible says *"choose this day life or death, blessing or cursing"* (Deuteronomy 30:19). Choose life!

Authority returned through the Last Adam (Jesus)

However, there is Good News! His name is Jesus! When He went to the cross, He disarmed satan and took back the power he had stolen, and the 'pecking order' was fundamentally changed forever. So, let's take some time now to clearly see what Jesus the Last Adam accomplished for us on the cross.

At this point it would be good to read Colossians 2:13-15, to help us understand all that was going on and how the Cross disarmed and destroyed the devil's hold over the believer in Christ. We can get a clear picture by considering the customs of the day. When a guilty man was crucified, a written charge or decree was hung over him, stating the crimes committed deserving death. Likewise, the 'written charge' of our sins, all deserving death, was nailed to the Cross of The Innocent One, Jesus. He paid the ultimate price to forgive our sins and take the wrath of God on Himself. Thus, enabling God to wipe away the record of decrees held against us, once and for all! (Colossians 2:14).

(The following Scriptures will help your further study: Romans 3:24-25, Hebrews 2:17, 1 John 2:2 and 1 John 4:10)

Depending on your bible translation, a key word from the above scriptures will keep popping up: Propitiation! It means to satisfy and appease. So, Jesus' death satisfied and appeased God, of His wrath and His justice. This is great news because God is now for us and not against us and satan no longer has any legal claims against us (Romans 8:1 and Romans 8:31).

As believers we are now seated with Christ in heavenly places, far
above all powers and dominions. Now Jesus commissions us to go in His Name and in His authority to bring man back to relationship with God, and back under the blessing which was God's plan from the beginning. [See Colossians 2:5, Matthew 28:18, Ephesians 1:3.]

This leads us to one of my favourite verses in the bible: 2 Corinthians 5:21 *'For He (God the Father) has made Him (Jesus) to be sin for us, who knew no sin, so that we might be made the righteousness of God in Him'*.

In conclusion, we can say that something remarkable happened at the cross. It is known as *'The Great Exchange.'* Jesus took all our sin, sickness, shame, sorrow and pain (Isaiah 53:4-5). In return He gave us His righteousness and His shalom (His peace). This righteousness is none other than the very righteousness of God. Wow! So now as a Christian, when God looks at us, He sees us just as righteous and blameless as Jesus!

CHAPTER SIX

THE NEW CREATION THROUGH JESUS
(the Last Adam)

Jesus' finished work on the cross, stripped satan of his legal right and hold over the believer. But it doesn't end there! The good news of the cross just keeps getting better and better. Under the order of the first Adam, satan had brought all of creation under his power of bondage and eternal death, but Jesus did something the devil never saw coming. Jesus made all who believe in Him a NEW CREATION! This is why we use the term 'Born again' or 'Born from above.'

2 Corinthians 5:17 *'Therefore, if anyone is in Christ, he is a new creation. The old has passed away; behold, the new has come.'* ESV

The original Greek renders the term 'New Creation', as *'A New Species of being.'* In other words a new type of creation, which until the cross had never existed upon planet Earth. In the Old Testament there were two people groups, Jews and Gentiles. Now in the New Testament we see a third group has emerged, the Church, comprising of new creation believers. So, just as Jesus died with His natural body, so must we, and like Jesus, we too are raised with an eternal body.

(For further study check out these scriptures... 1 Corinthians 15:47-54, 2 Corinthians 3:18, Romans 8:29 and 2 Peter 1:4.)

So, what has all this got to do with spiritual authority? Understanding the following foundational truths in Galatians will help us answer this question:

The four principles of our authority as believers.

(i) We have been crucified with Christ (Galatians 2:20)

It is very important to understand that the 'old you', the you before you were born again is long dead - two thousand years ago dead! Your old sinful nature including all manner of addictions, sorrow, sickness and demonic 'junk' was nailed to that 'old rugged cross' with Jesus and it's all NOW DEAD! So, don't be one of those Christians who fail to understand this truth, and live their lives in bondage to old ways of thinking and living.

(ii) He made us alive in Christ. (Ephesians 2:5)
Our old nature has been crucified, and NOW we have also been resurrected with Jesus to new life (Romans 8:11). We are alive, reborn, all fresh and new in the likeness of the Last Adam (1 Corinthians 15:45-49). We see this reality clearly in baptism. We go down into the water, which represents death with Christ and come up out of the water, which represents resurrection and new life.

(iii) He raised us up to heaven. (Ephesians 2:6)
Now that we are born again or born from above we have been raised up to heaven with Jesus, an important point to grasp, as we need to become 'ascended conscious.' In other words, we need to be living constantly in the reality of our birthright, choosing to live from heaven and all it's laws and principles, and not out of our old, earth bound Adamic nature.

(iv) He seated us with Christ. (Ephesians 2:6)
Okay, here is the big one! What does it mean to be seated with Christ? To answer this question we need to see exactly where Jesus is sitting (Ephesians 1:20-21), and that is at the right hand of the Father, far above all demonic and angelic authorities, powers and dominions. This verse tells us that we too are seated with Christ, and that means the answer to our question is - that in HIM, we are also way above all spiritual powers of darkness and all demons that reside on the earth and above the earth.

(For additional study see: Colossians 1:16, 2:15, 1Peter 3:22, Ephesians 3:10, Ephesians 2:2, Ephesians 6:12, Daniel 10:13 & 20, Isaiah 24:21.)

Jesus won back the authority

There are demonic forces working in our world and in the unseen realm of the second heaven. All unbelievers are under their authority, but now the demonic forces are subject to us, the believers seated with Christ in the third heaven. The body of Christ, His church, is truly a wonderful and powerful thing to behold. However, the church for the most part does not understand how powerful and how much authority she has at her disposal. The devil however, knows exactly what the church is capable of, so tries to keep the church in the dark in respect to her true identity.

Luke 10:19 *'I have given you authority to trample on snakes and scorpions and to overcome all the power of the enemy; nothing will harm you.'* NIV

So, in conclusion, the first Adam gave his authority to satan, legally making him the god of this world. Jesus, the Last Adam, took back that authority when He died and rose again. Now to all believers in HIM, He not only gave us earthly authority but also heavenly authority. Wow, praise God!

Matthew 28:18 *'And Jesus came and said to them, "All authority in heaven and on earth has been given to me.'* ESV

I hope you can see how much power you have against the devil and all his hordes of wickedness. Maybe it's time you cast the devil out of your life, your relationships, your finances, your health, your church, your addictions etc.

Mark 3:27 *'...Who is powerful enough to enter the house of a strong man like satan and plunder his goods? Only someone even stronger. Someone who could tie him up then plunder his house.'*

Now that you have Christ in you, you can now plunder the devil and finally stop him plundering you! (1 John 4:4 and James 4:7).

CHAPTER SEVEN

EXPULSION FROM THE BLESSING

Genesis 3:8 *'And they heard the voice of the LORD God walking in the garden in the cool of the day; and Adam and his wife hid themselves from the presence of the LORD God amongst the trees in the garden.'*

Here we begin to see the immediate effect of sin outworking itself and creating a barrier between man and God. Suddenly the beautiful loving Lord God becomes One to fear and hide from. The very nature of sin causes people to run away from God and tries to suppress the knowledge of Him. The further sinful man can get away from God's presence and His knowledge, the happier he thinks he will be. This is why we see the degradation of society as they pursue an agenda to become a godless generation (Isaiah 59:2, Romans 1:18 & 28-32, Romans 3:11-18).

Genesis 3:9 *'Then the Lord God called to the man, and said to him, "Where are you?"*. What a sad verse! But it is as relevant today as it was in the garden. God is still calling out to His creation: *"Where are you?"* Men and women are still cringing away from God in their sin, as they cannot cope with God's holy presence. The sadness of such a reaction is that people fear the very one who can save and spare them. The nature of sin twists and perverts man's nature to hate the very God whom he should naturally want to love.

A great example of this is in Isaiah Chapter 6, where Isaiah has a revelation of God Himself appearing to him. In verse 5 Isaiah cries out *'Woe is me for I am undone.'* To come face to face with God Almighty and to witness His glory, His majesty and His holiness is just too much for man to cope with. It is the sinful nature within man that makes him run and hide from such a God. Don't let it! Resist such responses at all costs.

We will see in Genesis 4 that this was the sin of Cain. He was angry and jealous that his brother's offering was accepted and his was rejected. The jealousy and pride in his heart perverted the love he had for his brother and turned him into a murderer. There is another similar story in 2 Samuel Chapter 13 where David's son Amnon falls in love with his half-sister Tamar. Amnon becomes so love sick, that in order to be alone with her, he asks her to bake him some cakes, then when she brings them to him, he rapes her. The love that he had felt for her turned instead to utter hatred. Guilt, shame, pride, and jealousy will do terrible things to the human heart. The scriptures tell us to guard our hearts above all things (Proverbs 4:23), and it is imperative that we do not allow such emotions to cloud us. If we do, we will find ourselves doing things we would never dream of doing.

But there is hope……………………

The first biblical prophecy (Jesus the Seed)

Genesis 3:15 *'And I will put enmity between you (satan) and the woman, and between **your seed and her seed**; He shall bruise your head and you shall bruise his heel.'* NASB

The theme of *'seed'* runs from Genesis to Revelation. It is an enormous study and one which would take many books to truly do it justice. Although this prophecy has great implications in many areas, first and primarily it is about Jesus. Then it expands out to us and other areas. So, let's look at this passage through the lens of it being about Jesus in the first instance.

In verse 15, we have the first prophecy in the bible referring to the Messiah, but note the two seeds - the seed of satan and THE SEED (singular) who is the Son of Man, the Son of God, Jesus. This verse also is an end-time prophecy stating the war between the antichrist and Jesus Christ. For both the seed of satan and the promise to Eve find their ultimate fulfilment in an individual. The seed of satan in the anti-christ (*pseudo-christ)*, and the seed of 'woman' finds fulfilment in the Christ, the Messiah.

Genesis 22:17-18 *"Indeed I will greatly bless you, and I will greatly multiply your seed as the stars of the heavens and as the sand which is on the seashore; and your seed shall possess the gate of their enemies. In your seed all the nations of the earth shall be blessed, because you have obeyed My voice."* NASB

To understand the wonderful revelation of this promise we need to decode it from the New Testament.

Galatians 3:16
Now the promises were spoken to Abraham and to his seed. He does not say, "And to seeds," as referring to many, but rather to one, "And to your seed," that is, Christ. NASB

So now let's look again at this passage of scripture, and I will paraphrase to make it really clear.

Genesis 22:17-18
"Indeed I will greatly bless you, and I will greatly multiply your seed (THE MESSIAH, JESUS) as the stars of the heavens and as the sand which is on the seashore; and your seed (THE MESSIAH JESUS AND HIS FOLLOWERS) shall possess the gate of their enemies. "In your seed (JESUS THE MESSIAH) all the nations of the earth shall be blessed, because you have obeyed My voice." NASB

Let's take a look at the first part of that passage: *'indeed I will greatly bless you, and I will greatly multiply your seed (THE MESSIAH, JESUS)'*.

As we saw in Chapter 2, the kingdom of God has the principle of expansion and multiplication embedded within it, i.e. you reap what you sow. Whatever we sow will always come back with more than we put in. First the natural then the spiritual. When we sow wheat in the ground we have a single seed. But that seed then bears a harvest of many seeds to each individual seed sown. This is teaching us the nature of God's kingdom. A single seed does not produce just another seed. No, an individual seed produces many seeds. It is a revelation on the earth of the heavenly law of God's nature and principles.

Matthew 13:33
'He told them still another parable: "The kingdom of heaven is like yeast that a woman took and mixed into about sixty pounds of flour until it worked all through the dough." NIV

Mark 4:8 *'Still other seed fell on good soil. It came up, grew and produced a crop, some multiplying thirty, some sixty, some a hundred times."* NIV

This is such a key principle that we really need to grasp. Indeed, in Mark chapter four the parable of the sower is called the key parable to understand all other parables (Mark 4:13). The principle of sowing and reaping is so profound and incredible that we should not take it for granted.

Genesis 26:12 *'Isaac planted crops in that land and the same year reaped a hundredfold, because the LORD blessed him.'* NIV

That means to every single seed he planted he got a hundred back.
So, if Isaac sowed a thousand seeds he would have got back a hundred thousand seeds. The hundredfold return is the maximum return you can get from a seed sown. This is made clear in the parable of the sower in Mark chapter 4:8

So back to Genesis 22:17 *'indeed I will greatly bless you, and I will greatly multiply your seed (THE MESSIAH, JESUS)...'*

Jesus is the ultimate Seed. He is The Seed with a capital 'S'! He is the Seed which gave birth to the new creation. He is the firstborn from the dead.

Colossians 1:18 *'He is also head of the body, the church; and He is the beginning, the firstborn from the dead, so that He Himself will come to have first place in everything.'* NASB

So, Jesus is the beginning. The beginning of what? The New Creation, the One New Man. Some people think that the One New Man is just a metaphor to Jew and Gentile living at peace with one another. Yes that is true, but it far, far transcends the metaphor. The One New Man is the New Creation, The Last Adam.

When Jesus died He went into the earth and like a seed gave birth to a new creation. Jesus literally went into the belly of the earth. He died, went into the ground physically and spiritually, then rose from the dead. But when He rose from the dead He was no longer mortal but immortal. He was the firstborn of a new species, a new creation to rise from the dead. The One New Man. In Whom Jew and Gentile can be made into something new which transcends cultural barriers, and which transcends our natural mortality. Thus, to become a Christian is to literally become BORN AGAIN or BORN ANEW into a new species, as we see in the following scriptures:

2 Corinthians 5:17
'Therefore if anyone is in Christ, he is a new creature(species); the old things passed away; behold, new things have come.' NASB

2 Corinthians 3:18
'But we all, with unveiled face, beholding as in a mirror the glory of the Lord, are being transformed into the same image from glory to glory, just as from the Lord, the Spirit.' NASB

1 Corinthians 15:47-54

'The first man is from the earth, earthy; the second man is from heaven. As is the earthy, so also are those who are earthy; and as is the heavenly, so also are those who are heavenly. Just as we have borne the image of the earthy, we will also bear the image of the heavenly. Now I say this, brethren, that flesh and blood cannot inherit the kingdom of God; nor does the perishable inherit the imperishable. Behold, I tell you a mystery; we will not all sleep, but we will all be changed, in a moment, in the twinkling of an eye, at the last trumpet; for the trumpet will sound, and the dead will be raised imperishable, and we will be changed. For this perishable must put on the imperishable, and this mortal must put on immortality. But when this perishable will have put on the imperishable, and this mortal will have put on immortality, then will come about the saying that is written, "DEATH IS SWALLOWED UP *in victory.'* NASB

Can you see the parallel here? Death is swallowed up in victory. As Jesus THE SEED died then rose again. So now we, as born again believers have the same spiritual DNA as Jesus within us so that when we die, we too rise again in an incorruptible, immortal body. Glory be to God for His wondrous wisdom!

2 Peter 1:4 *'For by these He has granted to us His precious and magnificent promises, so that by them you may become* **partakers of the divine nature**, *having escaped the corruption that is in the world by lust.'* NASB

I love that passage of scripture. We are partakers of His divine nature. That is so incredible. We have the same spiritual DNA as God. By saying this I am not stating that we are gods. I am stating that because of us being partakers of His divine nature we are now children of God.

John 1:12 *'But as many as received him, to them gave he power to become the sons of God, even to them that believe on his name:'* KJV

John 12:24-26 Truth Translation By Colin Urquhart: *'I tell you most emphatically, unless a seed of wheat falls into the ground and dies, it remains only a single seed...'*

When Jesus died on a cross, He didn't just die for our sins. He died to replicate Himself in a body of people who are filled with His Holy Spirit. Even some having to physically die so that the seeds of their martyrdom would cause and allow the church to continue to grow.

We are called to imitate and replicate Jesus' work upon the earth.

Ephesians 5:1 *'Imitate God, therefore, in everything you do, because you are his dear children.'* NLT

John 14:12 *'"I tell you the truth, anyone who believes in me will do the same works I have done, and even greater works, because I am going to be with the Father.'* NLT

CHAPTER EIGHT

THE BLESSING REVOKED THE CURSE PRONOUNCED

Genesis 3: 16-19 *"To the woman He said, I will greatly multiply your pain in childbirth, in pain you will bring forth children; yet your desire will be for your husband and he will rule over you. Then to Adam He said, because you have listened to the voice of your wife and have eaten from the tree about which I commanded you, saying, "You shall not eat from it." Cursed is the ground because of you; in toil you will eat of it all the days of your life. Both thorns and thistles it shall grow for you; and you will eat the plants of the field; By the sweat of your face you will eat bread, till you return to the ground, because from it you were taken; for you are dust and to dust you shall return."*

In these verses we see the blessing being revoked by God. And not just revoked - an 'anti-blessing', a curse is pronounced because of their rebellion. This is so sad because it has always been God's desire to bless His people, not curse them. Scripture makes it very clear that God looks for a man, woman or people group whom He can bless.

The curse can be summarised as a multiplication of sorrow: in conception, painful childbirth, disharmony between a man and woman, thorns and thistles to cause harm and grief, with work being hard and intensive. The effects of this curse are very much with us today in the modern world. To a degree, we have technology at our disposal to control the physical effects of the curse on the land, however, we know only too well that the 'thistles and weeds' can also spread and sprawl into our finances, our workplaces, into our churches, relationships and families. Sowing and reaping empowers the curse and its effects to just keep growing and spreading. But Jesus went to the cross to annul the effects of the curse!

Romans 8:19-22 *For the creation waits in eager expectation for the children of God to be revealed. For the creation was subjected to frustration, not by its own choice, but by the will of the one who subjected it, in hope. that the creation itself will be liberated from its bondage to decay and brought into the freedom and glory of the children of God. We know that the whole creation has been groaning as in the pains of childbirth right up to the present time.'* NIV

As we can apply the effects of salvation to our lives to break the power of the curse from which we have been redeemed, so also, we can pray God's redemption into the land and creation, which God has placed under our authority.

In Matthew 6:10 in the Lord's Prayer we are told to pray... *'Your Kingdom come, your will be done upon the earth, as it is being done right now in heaven.'*

In heaven there is no sadness, sickness or tears (Revelation 21:4). No death, no fear, no decay, no curse! So, when we see the effects of the curse trying to sprawl into our lives, finances, relationships etc, we have the right and authority to deal with it. The price has been paid in full for our redemption and the whole planet. So, apply it to your life and circumstances! Pray God's will and kingdom into every area of your life. Don't let the weeds and thorns of others creep into your household. Stop it dead by applying the blood to it! The blood of Jesus is the ultimate weed killer! His blood stops the curse dead. The price is paid in full. Believe it, live it, apply it! Walk in the blessing not the curse!

Remember, you are now a new creation in Christ. You no longer bear the image of the first Adam, but now take on the new image of the Last Adam. You are not subject to the curse! If you are born again, you are a new creation! (2 Corinthians 5:17) Do not be those who are *'destroyed for lack of knowledge'* (Hosea 4:6), but be transformed by the renewing of your mind by meditating on these truths. Be transformed by the truth, for it is the truth you know that will set you free! (Romans 12:1-2, John 8:32).

The Tree of Life

Genesis 3:22-24 *'Then the LORD God said, "Behold, the man has become like one of Us, knowing good and evil; and now, he might stretch out his hand, and take also from the tree of life, and eat, and live forever. therefore the LORD God sent him out from the garden of Eden, to cultivate the ground from which he was taken. So He drove the man out; and at the east of the garden of Eden He stationed the cherubim and the flaming sword which turned every direction to guard the way to the tree of life.'* NASB

As previously stated there were two very important trees in the garden: The tree of the knowledge of good and evil, which is the **Tree of Death** and the **Tree of Life.** It is ironic that after The Fall, this is the tree Adam and Eve were forbidden to eat from, the very tree which could have given them life. Oh, the pain of realisation for Adam and Eve when they perceived what they could have had! The devil cheated them out of the greatest treasure resulting in death through compromise and rebellion.

The devil still does this today - telling Christians to compromise, eat forbidden fruit now and repent later. The sad reality is that yes, God forgives, but the consequences of our actions may take longer to fix. We often forget this when we are being tempted. Yes, there is forgiveness and restoration, but there will be consequences. Consequences which could circumvent God's best for your life. Leave well alone the temptation to eat of the tree of death, wait till God gives you the fruit from the Tree of Life!

Earth and the third heaven have links that bind them together. There is a Mount Zion and Jerusalem in heaven (Hebrews 12:22, Revelation 21:2, Hebrews 11:9-10). This is a kingdom principle and mystery. The realms are supposed to be bound to one another, but satan is doing his very best to destroy the heavenly pattern from the earth to separate our world from the image of heaven. As man should reflect the glory of God so the earth should reflect the glory of heaven.

The Tree of Life was one of those links between heaven and earth. There was a Tree of Life on the earth and another in heaven (Genesis 3:22, Revelation 2:7, Revelation 22:2). Sadly, this link has now all but gone from the earth, but the good news is that we can still link the heaven to the earth, in Christ, who is our Tree of Life.

We have God's kingdom within us to live out in our earthly lives, (Luke 17:21). The role of the church upon the earth is to manifest the kingdom of heaven upon the earth. We are now trees of life to this dying world. We have within us The Seed of Life which is the gospel. The gospel is the power of God to salvation to those that believe (Romans 1:16). We are now the primary link between heaven and earth. For within us is the Holy Spirit who traverses the two realms. We are directly linked to heaven and this is why it is so imperative that we live out the heavenly pattern upon this dark, dead and diseased ridden planet. Let's show the world the beauty of the Tree of Life which comes through Jesus and His Holy Spirit.

In Genesis 3:24 the way to eternal life was shut up and closed. A new way was needed. Justification by faith alone. Now a simple faith in Jesus is what makes us righteous and born again. Jesus is The Way, The Truth and The Life. The way to the Tree of Life is no longer barred. We have eternal life through Jesus. We are seed carriers of this wonderful life and it's up to us to spread this seed wherever we go. We are salt and light to a bland and dark world. Let the church arise in these last days! Arise and shine for your light has come!

CHAPTER NINE

OFFERINGS TO GOD

Genesis 4:3-5 *'And in the process of time it came to pass, that Cain brought of the fruit of the ground an offering unto the Lord. And Abel, he also brought of the firstlings of his flock and of the fat thereof. And the Lord had respect unto Abel and to his offering; But unto Cain and to his offering he had not respect. And Cain was very wroth, and his countenance fell...'* KJV

Here in Genesis Chapter 4 we have an insight into the early days of life on earth after the fall. It seems that there was a form of harvest festival being celebrated, as both brothers brought an offering at the same time.

I have seen many commentaries on this passage that look at why God had respect for Abel's offering and not Cain's. Generally, some seem to focus on what was presented saying that Abel's gift was accepted because it was an animal sacrifice. However, even the law of Moses allows animals **and** crops to be presented before God as an acceptable offering of worship.

The simple difference between Abel and Cain in my opinion, was their heart condition in giving, which made the offering acceptable or not. Abel came with faith and expectancy. Cain came and gave just what was expected and required, we could say 'the way of religion'. They both looked the same outwardly but inwardly they were worlds apart.

The key to this passage is found in Hebrews 11:4 *'**BY FAITH** Abel offered to God a more excellent sacrifice than Cain offered. Through this (faith) he was approved as righteous...'*

We do not know how Cain knew that God was unhappy with his offering, but it is clear from the text that God had rejected it. Abel was a man who evidently loved God, whilst Cain just believed in God from a distance. A living faith in God is very different from being a religious believer. Just because you believe in God does not mean you have a ticket to heaven: James 2:19 *'You believe that there is one God. Good! Even the demons believe that--and shudder.'* NIV

Religious people believe in God, but a person of faith is one who not only believes but "knows God." John 17:3 states *'And this is eternal life, that they might **know You** the only true God, and Jesus Christ whom you have sent.'*

A living faith in God is so important when we come before Him. When we bring our lives as offerings to Jesus, our time, worship, financial gifts etc., we should always do so from a place of joy and faith, not going through the motions because our religion demands it. Come before God with boldness and thanksgiving in your heart and believe that He is the rewarder of those who seek Him! (Hebrews 4:16, Psalm 95:2, Hebrews 11:6).

Hate and murder are the same

Genesis 4:8 *'And Cain talked with Abel his brother; and it came to pass, when they were in the field, that Cain rose up against Abel his brother and slew him.'*

Here we start to see the fruit of the tree of knowledge of good and evil (tree of death) taking hold upon the earth, resulting in the first murder recorded in the bible. The text implies this murder was premeditated as Cain was chatting with Abel while taking him somewhere quiet from prying eyes. The nature of sin is revealed in Cain's actions. Because Abel's offering of faith was the one accepted, Cain wanted him dead rather than taking responsibility and dealing with his own feelings of rejection and inadequacy.

Now it's easy for us to sit here and pass judgement upon Cain for his actions, but in reality I am sure many of us are just as guilty as he is. Have we ever been angry with someone especially when they are in the right and we know we are in the wrong? In those moments we do one of two things: Admit our folly, or very likely just get angry and throw out a barrage of statements which point the blame away from ourselves.

Let's look at what the bible has to say about this kind of anger...

Matthew 5:22 *'But I tell you that anyone who is angry with a brother or sister will be subject to judgment. Again, anyone who says to a brother or sister, 'Raca,' is answerable to the court. And anyone who says, 'You fool!' will be in danger of the fire of hell.'* NIV

1 John 3:15 *'Anyone who hates a brother or sister is a murderer, and you know that no murderer has eternal life residing in him.'* NIV

Anger alone is not a sin. For example, we can be righteously angry at human slavery, or seeing people being treated unjustly. However, anger becomes a sin when it gets mixed with offence and is used as a smoke screen for us not dealing with our own issues and insecurities. When anger turns to hate then beware! Deal with it quickly by repenting and forgiving. Do not let a root of bitterness take hold!

Forgiveness is such a key element in all of this. The bible is very clear,
(Matthew 6:15 and Matthew 18:21-35) no matter how justified we may feel, we have to forgive. Because if we do not forgive others, God will not forgive us for our sins. So, what happens if you have been deeply wounded by someone and you just cannot forgive them? Well, firstly, you have to acknowledge that you <u>have to</u> forgive the one(s) who wronged you. Secondly, ask God to help you to forgive. Sometimes forgiveness can be a simple decision and the offence is dealt with, other times it's a process we have to walk through. The key is to be actively engaged with God, and to be assured that while you are working through the process, God knows your heart.

Our God is a kind, merciful and compassionate God. He will never fail or forsake you. (See Exodus 33:19 and Deuteronomy 31:8).

CHAPTER TEN

THE HIDDEN CODE OF SALVATION
THE WAY BACK TO BLESSING

Reading through the genealogies in the bible, may at first seem as exiting as reading through a telephone directory! But trust me, it is worth persevering! For example, in Genesis 5 a wonderful hidden code of God's plan of salvation to the world is clearly revealed in the 'generations of Adam'.

Here is the list of the names and their meanings.

Adam	Man
Seth	To place or appoint
Enosh	Mortal (misery, frail, sorrow)
Kenan	Immovable
Mahalalel	Blessed
Jared	To descend (will come down)
Enoch	Initiating (or to train, to teach)
Methuselah	His death will release
Lamech	Grieving
Noah	Rest.

Now let's put all these names into a sentence and see what appears.
"Man [is] appointed mortal sorrow. [But the] blessed will come down, teaching [that] His death will release [the] grieving [to] rest.

This prophecy coded here in Genesis 5 was fulfilled by Jesus, He spoke the words in Matthew 11:28 *'Come unto me, all you that labour and are heavy laden, and I will give you rest.'* Jesus became The Word made flesh, he died on the cross and through His blood we enter into this rest (Mark 14:61, John 1:14, Hebrews 4:10-11). What a wonderful God we serve! From the very beginning He was prophesying the coming blessing for the world, Jesus our Messiah! It clearly shows the manifold wonders of God's love, grace and favour toward us. Praise His Name!

CHAPTER ELEVEN

SEED TIME AND HARVEST

Genesis 8:22 *"While the earth remains, seedtime and harvest, and cold and heat, and summer and winter, and day and night shall not cease."* NASB

In this passage God is making it clear to Noah and to us, that as long as planet earth exists, certain natural laws will continue to operate. Even after the flood, the basics of sowing, reaping, seasons etc. will continue until the end of days. God will not change His mind on this matter. He decreed it to Noah and it's written in our bibles to encourage us. Remember, God is not a man that He should lie. He is unchanging and remains consistently the same. Glory be to His Name! (Numbers 23:19, Malachi 3:6, Psalm 102:25-27).

As mentioned before, there is a key principle in 1 Corinthians 15:46, *'first the natural and then the spiritual.'* As explained in chapter 2, all truth is parallel i.e. that which we can see in the natural is true in the spiritual. Therefore, we can sow and reap both to the flesh and to the Spirit. Each has obvious side effects, to the Spirit life and peace, to the flesh death and strife.

Galatians 6:8 *'Whoever sows to please their flesh, from the flesh will reap destruction; whoever sows to please the Spirit, from the Spirit will reap eternal life.'* NIV

Just as there are seasons of winter and summer, cold and hot, the church has also reflected these seasons of being cold in apathy, to being hot in revival. Let us always strive to be red hot in zeal and love for Jesus and His church! Scripture tells us that the worst kind of church is lukewarm (See Revelation 3:16). It is neither hot nor cold, neither alive nor dead. Therefore, as the world grows lukewarm to the things of God, let us make sure that we, the church, are always red hot for Him!

Additionally, there are natural and spiritual seasons. Ecclesiastes 3:1-8 reveals to us that there are times and seasons in the ways of man which need to be understood. Likewise, there are spiritual seasons that we need to recognize and flow with. 2 Timothy 4:2 tells us to preach the word of God in season and out of season. The Hebrew calendar, with all the Jewish feasts, reveals to us the different seasons in God's dealings with man past and future. Even the earth has spiritual days and nights. Look at what Jesus Himself says in John 9:4 *'As long as it is day, we must do the works of Him who sent Me. Night is coming, when no one can work.'* NIV

Scripture also shows us that when Jesus returns the world will be in a time of great spiritual darkness. 1 Thessalonians 5:2 *'For you know very well the **DAY** of the lord will come like a thief in the **NIGHT**.'*

We know from history that we have gone through periods of great darkness upon the earth. The 'Dark Ages' was a time in church history when it seemed that the truth and light of the gospel was almost snuffed out from existence. It was a time when the 'religion' of man prevailed upon the earth, however even in the darkest of places, God's glorious gospel endured.

CHAPTER TWELVE

GOD BLESSES NOAH

Gen 9:1-2 *"And God blessed Noah and his sons and said to them", "Be fruitful and multiply, and fill the earth, the fear of you and the terror of you will be on every beast of the earth and on every bird of the sky; with everything that creeps on the ground, and all the fish of the sea, into your hand they are given."*

In these verses God is blessing Noah and his sons, almost word for word the same as the blessing given to Adam and Eve. The heart of God is always to bless a people who are devoted to Him. If you are a believer in Jesus, you need to know that you are blessed right now! You may not feel it, or even look it, but you are! Indeed, God has blessed the believer with EVERY spiritual blessing. That means everything has been given in Christ for us to blessed.

Another point to note is, the blessing was always traditionally given to the man. Why was this? Well, it has to do with headship, responsibility and accountability (1 Corinthians 11:3, Ephesians 5:21-24). By God blessing the spiritual head of a household, the blessing would automatically belong to the women and children. It is passed down to them, via their husband who had received it from God. So, it is a real honour and delight for the fathers to pray for and speak blessing over their wives and children, by doing this they are imitating their spiritual head, who is God Himself.

If a man is failing in his family in some way spiritually, then it will be him, not the wife or children, who God will hold responsible. Remember, when Adam and Eve sinned it was Adam that God called for, and not Eve, because God wanted an explanation from the spiritual head. 1 Peter 3:7 states: *'In the same way, you husbands must give honour to your wives treat your wife with understanding as you live together. She may be weaker than you are, but she is your equal partner in*

God's gift of new life. Treat her as you should so your prayers will not be hindered.' NLT

So, are women just as blessed as men in the kingdom of God? Yes of course they are! Women are co-heirs in Christ together with the men, and just as blessed. Also, what happens if the family unit is being run by a widow, single or divorced lady? If there is no man to be a spiritual covering, then you go to the next one up which is Jesus Himself.

CHAPTER THIRTEEN

THE CALL OF ABRAM

Gen 12:1 *"Now God said to Abram", "Go forth from your country, and from your relatives, and from your Father's house, to the land which I will show you".*

God gives a clear call to Abram and tells him to leave his own county, his kin folk and his father's house. In fact, God is calling Abram out of worldliness to follow Him exclusively, as He tells him to leave behind everything, and go to a new land. Thus, begins Abram's incredible life of faith and adventure with God Almighty. Interestingly, he was 75 when God called him to leave his father's house (Gen 12:4). Suffice to say that we are never too young or too old to follow God when He calls us to do something for Him!

Archaeology verifies that in the Land of Ur and Haran, in Abram's day, many of the people worshiped the moon god. It was also a vibrant place of wealth and commerce. We can never say for sure, but Abram was probably very wealthy and comfortable in substance. So, when God called him to leave *everything*: it was a big ask! Regardless of the implications, Abram, like a brave pioneer, ventured out by faith. He set out following a God who speaks and lives, not knowing where he would really end up.

God asked Abram to go into a land that He would disclose to him when he arrived. This land was ultimately Israel in the natural, but as Abram settled, he also dwelt there in faith and expectation of seeing the TRUE PROMISED LAND.

Hebrews 11:8-10 *'By faith Abraham obeyed when he was called to go out into a place which he would later receive as an inheritance. He went out not knowing where he was going. By faith he dwelt in the promised land as in a foreign land, dwelling in tents with Isaac and Jacob, the heirs of the* *same promise, **for he was looking for a city which has foundations whose builder and maker is God.'*** MEV

So, in the process of his journey in the natural, God revealed to Abram the heavenly destination for all those who follow the pathway of faith. God was leading Abram on the path of revelation and ultimately to salvation. God has the same calling for us today. Yes, He wants many to come to know Him as their Lord and Saviour, but He also wants His people to come into a 'land' of joy and intimacy through revelation.

In the apostle Paul's letter to the Ephesians, he prays that God would give them *'The Spirit of wisdom and revelation in the knowledge of Him, that the eyes of their understanding may be enlightened, that they may know what is the hope of their calling'* Ephesians 1:17-18. This is what every believer should be praying for! Revelation and intimacy are divinely connected, one leads to the other, and empowers us to grow in the knowledge of God. This is His desire that His people would know Him and His ways through relationship. This is the wonderful privilege given to the believer. John 17:3 states that *'eternal life is knowing God.'*

CHAPTER FOURTEEN

THE BLESSING OF ABRAHAM Part 1

Genesis 12:2 *'"I will make you into a great nation, and I will bless you; I will make your name great, and you will be a blessing.'* NIV

Let's compare this to the blessing given to Adam and Eve

Genesis 1:28 *'And God blessed them. And God said to them, "Be fruitful and multiply and fill the earth and subdue it, and have dominion over the fish of the sea and over the birds of the heavens and over every living thing that moves on the earth."* NASB

In comparing Genesis 1 and 12 we can see there are similarities. God wants His people to grow, expand and spread across the earth; to be blessed, to have great favour, to have dominion and influence. However, the Abrahamic blessing ends on a different note, in that God want His people to be like Him and be the source of blessing to others. This is why He calls us to be a light to the gentiles/nations (Acts 13:47, Isaiah 42:6), as we are carriers of God Almighty, His Gospel, and His Kingdom within us (1 John 4:4, Matthew 28:16-20, Luke 17:21). We can lay hands on the sick and see them healed (Mark 16:17-18). We can tell people the wonders of God and His beautiful Son and lead people into eternal life. Also, because the love of God abounds in our hearts, we can show practical love to our fellow man through acts of kindness and generosity.

We should also be atmosphere changers. We have the kingdom of God within us! When we walk into a room we should not fear the darkness in man. On the contrary we should know that when we walk into a room we are carriers of God's kingdom and power. As a carrier we need to infect people with the light God has given us. He wants us to be like Him in that we separate the light from the darkness. We are called to separate people from darkness to His glorious light (1 Peter 2:9).

This is what the Gospel is all about. Separating light from darkness, sheep from goats, wheat from tares. We are instruments of salvation and healing to the world. God really wants us to understand that we are not here on the earth just as an inconvenience to society, a mere religion with no power. No! We are children of Almighty God and He has commissioned us to do exploits in His Name, and by His power we *will* bring many from darkness into light. As we have freely received, so we should freely give.

The bible teaches us that it is more blessed to give than to receive (Acts 20:35). When we 'sow' the blessing that God has given us to others, we in turn, will always 'reap' a greater blessing. Why? Because it shows the nature of our Father in heaven, and we feel His pleasure as we seek to imitate Him (Ephesians 5:1).

CHAPTER FIFTEEN

THE BLESSING OF ABRAHAM Part 2

Genesis 12:2 *"'I will make you into a great nation, and I will bless you; I will make your name great, and you will be a blessing."* NIV

When we read a scripture verse like this one, it is tempting to use our Greek mindset of 'compartmentalising' and come to the conclusion that it applies to Abraham and those "other guys," of a time long ago.

Galatians 3:29 confirms that the people group and nation referred to in Gen 12:2, includes us believers! *'If you belong to Christ, then you are Abraham's seed, and heirs according to the promise.'* NIV

We are Abraham's seed and thus his children. Therefore, we come under the same blessings pronounced upon him.

Galatians 3:8-9 *'Scripture foresaw that God would justify the Gentiles by faith, and announced the gospel in advance to Abraham: "All nations will be blessed through you." So those who rely on faith **are blessed along with Abraham**, the man of faith.'* NIV

God wants to bless us so that we can be a blessing to those around us, but we have to start accepting this truth by faith and throw away the lies and teachings of men and tradition. God wants all His children blessed so that we can be a blessing to those around us.

Still not convinced? Look at this passage from the Amplified bible...
2 Corinthians 9:8 *'And God is able to make all grace (every favour and earthly blessing) come to you in abundance, so that you may always and under all circumstances and whatever the need be self-sufficient [possessing enough to*

require no aid or support and furnished in abundance for every good work and charitable donation.]'

God spoke out His promise to make Abraham 'a great nation' making him the father of the circumcised and the father of those who believe by faith. So, from Abraham comes an innumerable host made up of the natural and spiritual people of God (Romans 4:11-12), both partakers of the same promise. Through circumcision we have the natural blood line of the Jewish race, and through the way of faith, all those who believe in Jesus:

Ephesians 3:6 *'This mystery is that through the gospel the Gentiles are heirs together with Israel, members together of one body, and sharers together in the promise in Christ Jesus.'* NIV

Every individual starting from Abraham has the opportunity to be a source of fulfilment to the promise of becoming a great nation. Every person we lead to the Lord becomes a child of that great promise. Every child that grows up in the way of faith is a member of that great nation. Today in our churches and ministries we are all making a difference in growing that great nation.

Psalm 127:1 states: *'Unless the LORD builds the house, those who build it labor in vain. Unless the LORD watches over the city, the watchman stays awake in vain.'* ESV

We are blessed to be a blessing. We are blessed by God through the promise, and we are blessed and empowered by God to fulfil the promise.

Genesis 12:3 *'I will bless those who bless you, and whoever curses you I will curse; and all peoples on earth will be blessed through you.'"* NIV

This is a wonderful passage of scripture. However, the thought that God curses those who curse us may seem alien to our thinking. After all, Jesus teaches that we should love those who hate and persecute us, love thy neighbour etc. Actually, both are true. Our job is to bless those who hate us, it is God who does the blessing and cursing and not us. Look again at this passage...

'I will bless those who bless you, and whoever curses you I will curse; and all peoples on earth will be blessed through you."' NIV

Our job is to show the world the love and compassion of God even in times of intense opposition and persecution. The idea of God cursing our enemies even while we bless them, is not so far removed as you may think: Romans 12:19-20 states *'Do not take revenge, my dear friends, but leave room for God's wrath, for it is written: "It is mine to avenge; I will repay," says the Lord. On the contrary: "If your enemy is hungry, feed him; if he is thirsty, give him something to drink. In doing this, you will heap burning coals on his head."'* NIV

Remember, we are blessed to be a blessing. So that is what we must keep doing. Be a blessing and bless! We don't get to pick and choose who is worthy of the blessing. We bless all humanity. We especially bless those who hate us. There was probably a time when you and I hated God. Yet He chose to keep blessing us until that wonderful day came, when our hearts melted so we could accept His free offer of salvation.

It is God's will that none should perish (2 Peter 3:9), so to recap, we need to be agents of blessing, salt and light, which the world is waiting for and so desperately needs in these dark last days.

CHAPTER SIXTEEN

ABRAHAM WAS RICH

Genesis 13:2 *'And Abram was very rich in cattle, in silver and in gold.'* KJV

There are several teachings within the bible which the church, for the most part, has chosen to ignore. In my opinion, this is because of the stigma attached to them, together with basic misunderstanding. A deep-seated suspicion of God prospering His people, comes from church teaching originating from the middle ages by the Catholic and early reformation movement. The notion that God wants to prosper us is almost an obscene notion to some, but the bible is full of passages regarding God's blessing of covenantal Shalom (peace) and Chesed (His covenantal loving kindness) toward us. Our natural minds cannot even begin to fathom the depths of our riches in Christ and the inheritance He has given to us (see Ephesians 1:3, Ephesians 3:8, 1 Peter 1:4, Romans 8:17).

God has given us such wonderful riches in Christ Jesus, a wonderful inheritance and has blessed us with every spiritual blessing in heaven.
The problem with SUPER SPIRITUALISING is that it sanitises the power of the cross. Some may look at the blessings upon Abraham and Israel and see them as physical blessings only and likewise consider the New Testament blessings as spiritual only. Believe it or not, this kind of thinking is a form of gnosticism which is actually heresy. Gnosticism is a philosophy that teaches anything to do with the flesh is evil and anything to do with the spirit is good.

When Jesus died on the cross, He came to save **THE WHOLE MAN**, spirit, soul and body. Many Christians think that when we die we just go to heaven in a spiritual realm forever. This is completely contrary to scripture, as God has promised us a new resurrection body on the last day. Now, if we just float around heaven for all eternity why did Jesus promise a resurrection from the dead with a new physical body which is immortal at the last day upon the earth? Because we are not going to stay in heaven.

Let's look at some scriptures to clarify this...
John 11:23-24, Daniel 12:13, John 6:40, 1 Corinthians 15:23, 1 Thessalonians 4:14-17.

Another key scripture is found in Revelation 21:1-3 *'Then I saw a new heaven and a new earth, for the first heaven and the first earth had passed away, and the sea was no more. And I saw the holy city, new Jerusalem, coming down out of heaven from God, prepared as a bride adorned for her husband. And I heard a loud voice from the throne saying, "Behold, the dwelling place of God is with man. He will dwell with them, and they will be his people, and God himself will be with them as their God."'* ESV

Notice there will be a new heaven and a new earth. Now did you see that? A new planet called earth and the City of God, New Jerusalem actually comes down out of heaven and lands on the new planet earth.
In other words, we don't stay in heaven for ever. No, indeed at some point in the future when Jesus returns we are given an immortal flesh body, for eternity.

God created us tripartite - we have a spirit, soul and body. If we died today only our spirit and soul would go to heaven. But one day, the last day, we will be given a new body which will allow us to live upon the new planet earth, where God will descend from heaven and dwell with man forever (Revelation 21:1-3).

Resurrection of the dead???

Bear with me…….!

The doctrine of the resurrection of the dead is a preliminary basic teaching every church should embrace (Hebrews 6:1-3).

However, many churches infrequently mention it, even those that do, rarely link it to the rapture of the church at the end of days. The rapture is not just about the taking away of the church, rather it's also about the resurrection of the dead! Paul explains this well in I Thessalonians 4:16-18: *'For The Lord Himself will descend from heaven with a shout, with the voice of the archangel and with the trumpet of God, and the dead in Christ will rise first. Then we who are alive and remain will be caught up together with them in the clouds to meet The Lord in the air, and so we shall always be with The Lord'*.

The bible speaks of two resurrections - one on the last day when Jesus returns (Revelation 20:4-6 and John 6:40) and one at the end of the millennial reign of Jesus upon the earth, with a resurrection unto judgement for non-believers (Revelation 20:12-13 and John 5:29).
A simple rule of thumb is 'let the scripture speak for itself.' Do not add or subtract.

So, getting back to the point of this chapter that Abraham was rich, any blessing from God should be a blessing to the whole man as we see in 3 John 1:2 *'Beloved, I wish above all things that you may prosper and be in health as your soul prospers.'*

The condition of our soul will have an effect on the whole man, body, soul and spirit. Man is a complete being and should be treated as such. If he is sick in soul or spirit or flesh it will affect all of him. To say that Jesus came to give us life and life in abundance, but only in the spiritual is a complete misunderstanding of the nature of salvation. If God doesn't care for our bodies why did Jesus heal so many people? Why did He promise us a new resurrection body? It is because He does care. He made us tripartite not bipartite (i.e. not just a spirit and soul).

So, what has all this got to do with God blessing and prospering us? Well, it has everything to do with it. We need to dismantle wrong thinking with the aid of scripture. If you think it's wrong for God to bless you in this natural world, it is basically down to a misunderstanding of the nature of your salvation and scripture. Christ died to save the whole man, not just a part of you. All of you! Why? Because God created you in His image, tripartite, and tripartite you will remain!

So, in conclusion, your spirit man is saved, your soul is being saved and your body will be saved at the final day.

CHAPTER SEVENTEEN

THE BLESSING OF ABRAHAM Part 3

Psalm 33:12 *'Blessed is the nation (people group) whose God is the LORD, the people whom He has chosen for His own inheritance.'* NASB

When a nation submits to God and His word that nation is blessed. How is it blessed? Well, for example, protection from enemies, expansion of territories, influence, economic growth etc. Deuteronomy 28:1-14 lists some of the blessings which God gave to His people Israel. Now this takes us to the next point of error. There are many believers who have no problem in believing that the Jewish people are a nation blessed above all other nations. Yet many of the same Christians fail to see that they are grafted into Israel and have the same covenantal benefits, if not more so than natural Israel.

Let's look again at a few key scriptures…..

Genesis 12:2-3 *'And I will make you a great nation, And I will bless you, and make your name great; And so you shall be a blessing; And **I will bless those who bless you, And the one who curses you I will curse**. And in you all the families of the earth will be blessed."*
NASB

Genesis 35:11 *'God also said to him, "I am God Almighty; Be fruitful and multiply; A nation and **a company of nations shall come from you**, And kings shall come forth from you.'*
NASB

So, in Genesis 12:2-3 it states that God will bless those who bless you and curse those who curse you. Who does this apply to? Israel only? Genesis 35:11 states very clearly that a company of nations shall come from Abraham. But who are the other nations? The other nations are the gentiles, and that includes us!

Galatians 3:7 *'Therefore, be sure that it is those who are of faith who are sons of Abraham.'* NASB
If you believe in Jesus then you are a child of Abraham. Romans 4:9-12 reveals that Abraham is the father of the circumcised and the father of those who believe through faith.

Ephesians 2:11-13 & 19 *'Therefore, remember that formerly you who are gentiles by birth and called "uncircumcised" by those who call themselves "the circumcision" (which is done in the body by human hands)-remember that at that time you were separate from Christ, excluded from citizenship in Israel and foreigners to the covenants of the promise, without hope and without God in the world. But now in Christ Jesus you who once were far away have been brought near by the blood of Christ. Consequently, you are no longer foreigners and strangers, but fellow citizens with God's people and also members of his household.'* NIV

We were once estranged from God and His covenants but now, as believers according to verse 19, we are no more estranged, but are fellow citizens with Israel. So, let's get this fact straight. A gentile believer can be as blessed physically as the Jewish person. The quicker the church understands that she is grafted into Israel, the faster she will understand that her blessings are not just merely spiritual, but also physical. So now the church is also a light to the gentiles. Why? Because we are the blessed people of God who have the gospel of eternal life to give to all who would receive it.

CHAPTER EIGHTEEN

THE BLESSING OF ABRAHAM Part 4

It may come as a surprise to some, but in the creation account in Genesis, God did not say "it was good," seven times. It was actually eight. The eighth time appears in Genesis 2:12

'And the gold of that land is good.' KJV

Now let's look at Genesis 13:2

*'Now Abram was very rich in livestock, in silver and in **gold**.'* NASB

Another scripture of note is Psalm 35:27

'Let them shout for joy and rejoice, who favour my vindication; And let them say continually, "The LORD be magnified, **Who delights in the prosperity of His servant**.*"* NASB

The word here for prosperity in the Hebrew, is the word *Shalom*. This is why various bible translations will treat the word differently. *Shalom* is a powerful word and a wonderful gift God has given to man that can only come through covenant with God Himself. *Shalom* denotes God's prosperity, wholeness, health, vitality, life, abundance, peace, joy and so much more. We see similar renderings of Greek words in the New Testament which are Greek equivalents to the word *Shalom*.

John 10:10 *'The thief comes only to steal and kill and destroy. I came that they may have **life** and have it abundantly.'* ESV

The Greek word for *Life* in this text is 'Zoe'. This is 'abundant life', full of vitality, energy and hope. The word is often linked to healing and salvation. Like *Shalom* it denotes God's abundance toward us through His grace.

Another interesting verse in the New Testament is found in 3 John 1:2.

*'Beloved, I wish above all things that you may **prosper** and be in **health** even as your soul prospers'* KING JAMES 2000 VERSION

It is a sad state of affairs when many Christians live in bondage and under the curse of the law, simply because they do not understand that they should now be living in the blessing of God. A lot of people choose to live under the curse simply because they honestly and humbly believe that is where God wants them to be. Too many Christians are in poverty, lack, sickness, and frustration, simply because they do not understand that they have been redeemed from the curse and are now in Christ, receivers of the blessing of Abraham.

Let's read our key scripture again:
Galatians 3:13-14 *'But Christ has rescued us from the curse pronounced by the law. When He was hung on the cross, He took upon Himself the curse for our wrongdoing. For it is written in the Scriptures, "Cursed is everyone who is hung on a tree." Through Christ Jesus, God has blessed the Gentiles with the same blessing He promised to Abraham, so that we who are believers might receive the promised Holy Spirit through faith'* NLT.

Also take a moment to look again at Genesis 12:1-3.
'Now the LORD said to Abram, "Go forth from your country, and from your relatives and from your father's house, To the land which I will show you; and I will make you a great nation, and I will bless you, and make your name great; and so you shall be a blessing; and I will bless those who bless you, and the one who curses you I will curse. And in you all the families of the earth will be blessed" NASB.

It needs to be made clear that this blessing is as much for you and me as it is for the Jew. It is for all those in the family of

Abraham. We are members of his family through faith in Christ.

Galatians 3:29 *'And if you belong to Christ, then you are Abraham's descendants, heirs according to promise'* NASB.

In the days of Jesus, the holy temple had an area known as the 'Court of the Gentiles.' It was in this area that Jesus drove out all the money changers (John 2:15). He was 'righteously angry' because the Gentiles were being denied the right to pray and worship God. This court of the Gentiles was separated so that Jew and Gentile could never mix. However, Jesus has now taken away this partition wall. The following scriptures explain this:

Galatians 3:28   *'There is neither Jew nor Greek, there is neither slave nor free, there is no male and female, for you are all one in Christ Jesus.'* ESV

Ephesians 2:12-13 *'In those days you were living apart from Christ. You were excluded from citizenship among the people of Israel, and you did not know the covenant promises God had made to them. You lived in this world without God and without hope. But now you have been united with Christ Jesus. Once you were far away from God, but now you have been brought near to him through the blood of Christ.'* NLT

Ephesians 2:14-15 *'For Christ himself has brought peace to us. He united Jews and Gentiles into one people when, in His own body on the cross, He broke down the wall of hostility that separated us. He did this by ending the system of law with its commandments and regulations. He made peace between Jews and Gentiles by creating in Himself one new people from the two groups.'* NLT

Do you see it now? All the bible, all its blessings and promises are all yours! All of it! This is the glorious covenant and gospel we have received from God. All praise, glory and honour goes to His Name! Amen.

Now we understand that Christ has redeemed us from the curse of the law. It now stands to logical reason that if the power of the curse is broken, then the power of the blessing is released upon us. We have been redeemed from the curse of the law into the blessing. God's blessing upon us comes only through His covenant with us. We are the seed of Abraham and thus now enjoy the benefits of that covenant.

CHAPTER NINETEEN

ABRAM MEETS MELCHIZEDEK

Genesis 14:18-20   *'And Melchizedek King of Salem brought out bread and wine; now he was a priest of God Most High. He blessed him and said, "Blessed be Abram of God Most High, Possessor of heaven and earth; And blessed be God Most High, Who has delivered your enemies into your hand." He gave him a tenth of all.'* NASB

Every now and then the bible throws a 'curve ball' and takes us by surprise. The revealing of Melchizedek is such a one, and needless to say, a revelation of paramount importance. The best way to help us understand this passage is to break it down verse by verse.

(i) Firstly, let's look at the meaning of the name 'Melchizedek'. It is made of three components: 'Melchi' comes from the Hebrew word 'Melek' which means king; the 'i' of Melchi means 'my', and 'Zedek' comes from the Hebrew word 'tsedek' which means righteousness. So, the name Melchizedek literally translated means 'my King is righteousness.'

(ii) Next, we see his title 'King of Salem'. Now, 'Salem' is a component of the name Jerusalem which means city of peace, and comes from the Hebrew word 'Shalom,' which means peace, prosperity, wholeness, welfare and tranquility.

So, the full rendering of 'Melchizedek King of Salem' reads like this... *'My King of Righteousness; The King of prosperity, peace, wholeness, welfare and tranquility.'*

(iii) In the title 'Priest of God Most High' we are introduced to the priesthood of Melchizedek, which is an eternal priesthood, preceding and far superior to the Aaronic (Levitical) order. In his priestly role, as he met with Abram, Melchizedek, brought out bread and wine, the language of covenant.

It doesn't take a genius to figure out who Melchizedek is. He is very likely the pre-incarnate Son of God, Jesus!

(iv) Now, let's look at the meeting between Abram and Melchizedek, and the New Testament account in Hebrews 7:1 *'For this Melchizedek, king of Salem, priest of the Most High God, met Abraham returning from the slaughter of the kings and **blessed him** (Abraham)'* NASB.

At the time of their meeting, we could think that Abram was the superior one, as he had already been blessed by God and was a very significant and influential man. However, this was not the case, it is Melchizedek who is superior and gives the blessing.

Genesis 14:19 *'He blessed him and said, "**Blessed** be Abram of God Most High, **Possessor of heaven and earth**...'* NASB

Hebrews 7:6-7 *'But the one whose genealogy is not traced from them (Melchizedek) collected a tenth from Abraham and blessed the one who had the promises. But without any dispute the lesser is blessed by the greater.'* NASB

We see proof of Melchizedek's identity here. Abram was the one (a) blessed by God (b) to be a blessing and (c) the one to give a blessing, but at their meeting he was the lesser, being blessed by Melchizedek, 'the greater'. This is JESUS THE BLESSED ONE! the source of the blessing and the transferor of the blessing!

Later in the book of Genesis, Abram gets the full revelation of who Melchizedek is. He is the Word of the Lord.

Genesis 15:1-2 *'After these things **The Word of the LORD** came to Abram in a vision: "Fear not, Abram, I am your shield; your reward shall be very great." But Abram said, "**O Lord GOD**, what will you give me, for I continue childless, and the heir of my house is Eliezer of Damascus?"* ESV

Wow! this is an incredible passage. The Word of the Lord appears to Abram and starts to speak to him. The amazing part is Abram's reply to The Word of God. *"O Lord GOD..."* Abram immediately recognises The Word of God as none other than God Himself. This is Jesus! The Word of God who became flesh and dwelt amongst us.

Jesus is The Word of God...

John 1:1 *'In the beginning was the Word, and the Word was with God, and the Word was God...*

John 1:17 *'The Word became flesh and made His dwelling among us. We have seen His glory, the glory of the One and only Son, who came from the Father, full of grace and truth...'*

Let's look at how blessed Abram was in his day...

Abram was *'Possessor of heaven and earth...'* Now when we read the text in Genesis 14, we assume that the possessor of heaven and earth is God. This is true, but the context of the text is implying that Abram is also possessor of heaven and earth as a prophetic type of Christ. Some may feel I am stretching the text here, so let's look at the New Testament....

Romans 4:13 *'For the promise to Abraham and his offspring **that he would be heir of the world** did not come through the law but through the righteousness of faith.'* NASB

Hebrews 11:9-10 *'By faith he (Abraham) made his home in the promised land like a stranger in a foreign country; he lived in tents, as did Isaac and Jacob, who were heirs with him of the same promise. **For he was looking forward to the city with foundations, whose architect and builder is God**.'* NIV

Through this book we have been tracking *'The Blessing of Abraham'*- a blessing that is not just any kind of blessing! It is **THE BLESSING!** It is a specific blessing given by God to Abraham so that he would be blessed and be a blessing to the nations. Indeed, this blessing would empower Abraham's children (the Jewish nation and the church) to reflect the goodness of God upon the earth, so that we would be a light to the Gentiles.

Our light is our witness. The witness is not just simply telling people about Jesus. Our witness is that we are blessed and everyone knows it. The nations should look at the church in wonder, they should see that God is with us and not with them. Why? Because we are in covenant with God and they are not. Because we are in relationship with God through Christ, we are grafted into *THE BLESSING*.

The nation of Israel in the Old Testament was a blessed nation, and they were supposed to be a great nation, a powerful nation, a wealthy nation. They were to be a set apart people who had the presence of God in their very midst. This should be true of the church today as we are grafted into that same covenant (Galatians 3:14-15 & 29).

Genesis 14:19 *'**He blessed him** and said, "**Blessed** be Abram of God Most High, Possessor of heaven and earth"*. NASB

The Blessing is about the transfer of God's covenantal favour and power to establish His promises and kingdom upon the earth through mankind. This is the same blessing which the church should be happy to embrace today. It is not some nice greeting by God to Abram, this blessing is the key to God's plans and purposes being manifested upon the earth. He empowers His people to get wealth to establish the covenant upon the earth.

Deuteronomy 8:18 *'"But you shall remember the LORD your God, for it is He who is giving you **power** to make wealth,* *that He may <u>confirm</u> His covenant which He swore to your fathers, as it is this day.'* NASB

Deuteronomy 8:18 *'But thou shalt remember the LORD thy God: for it is He that giveth thee power to get wealth, that He may <u>establish</u> His covenant which He sware unto thy fathers, as it is this day.'* KJV

The Blessing not only empowers us to **establish** The Covenant, but it also **confirms** The Covenant. So, for the church to be walking in The Blessing, albeit in varying degrees, confirms the promises to the fathers. What fathers? Abraham, Isaac and Jacob!

By choosing to live under The Blessing and accepting it by faith, we are honouring and confirming the covenant of Abraham of which we are grafted into. We need to constantly remember, the point of The Blessing is to save mankind! The establishing of The Blessing in our lives not only testifies to the goodness of God individually and corporately, but also establishes from generation to generation God's redemptive plan upon the earth. The fulness of The Blessing will be manifest on the day Jesus returns and brings heaven down upon the earth. Then, finally The Blessing will be complete in the new heavens and the new earth when God dwells with man for ever and ever. Praise His Holy Name!

Genesis 14:20 *'and blessed be God Most High, **who has delivered your enemies into your hand!"** And Abram gave him a tenth of everything.'* ESV

Now in this verse we are seeing a precursor to a later blessing given to Abraham in Genesis 22:17 *"I will surely bless you, and I will surely multiply your offspring as the stars of heaven and as the sand that is on the seashore. And your offspring **shall possess the gate of his enemies**."* ESV

In Genesis 14 it is God Most High who has given a great victory to Abram alone, but in Genesis 22:17 the promise of victory against the enemy is given to <u>all his offspring</u>. So, for those who choose to walk by faith in The Blessing, can have this victory and possess the gates of their enemies.

This is made very clear in Luke 10:19 *"I have given you authority to trample on snakes and scorpions and to overcome all the power of the enemy; nothing will harm you."* NIV

Jesus is now sitting at the right hand of the Father (Ephesians 1:20-21). As Christians we need to note well that we too, are seated with Christ in heavenly places (Ephesians 2:6), and have been given a position of authority far above all powers and principalities and angelic dominions. Being 'seated' also denotes a finished work in which we have to rest by faith (Hebrews 4:10-11). Remember also that Jesus disarmed all the demonic host, that is not to say the enemy is powerless, rather, that his weapons are ineffective against us if we raise up our shield of faith and walk in the victory wrought through the Blood of Jesus (Ephesians 6:16).

CHAPTER TWENTY

THE TITHE

Genesis 14:20

*"And praise be to God Most High, who delivered your enemies into your hand." Then Abram **gave him a tenth of everything**.* NIV

Here we see Abraham giving Melchizedek (Jesus) tithes of all he had, a common thing to do in the ancient East and practiced long before the Law of Moses, as we see in the lives of the Patriarchs. One key theme of 'The Blessing' is that tithing is nearly always linked to it.

Tithing in the period of the Patriarchs was given voluntarily from a place of faith and thanksgiving. The tithe under the Law of Moses was demanded from the people to help pay for the priesthood and to help the poor.

When we get to the New Testament we run into difficulties with tithing. Partly because we find the concept of law and grace difficult to understand and thus we encounter problems of application. So, what does Jesus say? Well He encourages us to tithe and even go way beyond the tithe, (Matthew 23:23, 19:21, 18:22). However, there are those who state that Jesus was talking to people who are under the Law of Moses. This is a fair comment, for example, the ten lepers healed by Jesus, were encouraged to '*go and show themselves to the priests*' according to the Mosaic system (Luke 17:11-19). However, there is another scripture which puts an interesting slant on this:

Luke 16:16 *'"**The Law and the Prophets** were proclaimed until John. Since that time, the good news of the kingdom of God is being preached, and everyone is forcing their way into it.'* NIV

The Law and the Prophets, were preached until the last of the Old Testament prophets: John the Baptist. When Jesus came onto the scene He began preaching the New Way of the Kingdom of God. In other words, Jesus is now revealing a New Administration, the New Messianic Covenant, the Melchizedek administration, which was prophesied in Jeremiah 31:31 *'"The days are coming," declares the LORD, "when I will make a new covenant with the people of Israel and with the people of Judah.'* NIV

Hebrews 7:17-18 *'For it is declared: "You are a priest forever, in the order of Melchizedek." The former regulation (Mosaic Administration) is set aside because it was weak and useless.'* NIV

I think that the greatest misunderstanding of the New Testament is that we are not just under a New Covenant but also a New Administration, a new and better Priesthood. There are Christians who seek to live under the Law of Moses, because they love God's Word and His holy Law. Although I can understand why they seek to do this, we can see from the above verse that the former Mosaic Administration is weak and useless. Why is it useless?

Romans 8:3 *'For God has done what the law, weakened by the flesh, could not do. By sending his own Son in the likeness of sinful flesh and for sin, he condemned sin in the flesh,'* ESV

The law was weakened by our flesh. According to Romans 7 verses 5 onwards, Paul writes that the Law is holy and good, but it was our sinful nature which took the commandment and twisted that which should have brought life, and turned it to death. So, when the Law says *'You shall not covet,'* our sinful nature took that commandment and twisted it so that the flesh desired to covet. The very Law which is holy and good was perverted and made weak by the flesh. Romans 7:8 states *'But sin, taking opportunity through the commandment, pro-*

duced in me coveting of every kind; for apart from the Law sin is dead.' NASB

Romans 7:10 *'and this commandment, which was to result in life, proved to result in death for me;'* NASB

Romans 7:13 *'Therefore did that which is good become a cause of death for me? May it never be! Rather it was sin, in order that it might be shown to be sin by effecting my death through that which is good, so that through the commandment sin would become utterly sinful.'* NASB

The Law is good and holy. Man is sinful, perverts the commandment and is judged by the Law. So where does our hope lie? Our hope is with Jesus who fulfilled the Law. Through His fulfilment we, as believers, are clothed in His righteousness. His righteousness is in part His fulfilment and observance of the Law. So, when God looks upon the believer, He sees someone who has fulfilled the Law and is blameless and righteous.

2 Corinthians 5:21 *'He made Him who knew no sin to be sin on our behalf, so that we might become the righteousness of God in Him.'* NASB

Colossians 1:22 *'Yet now He has reconciled you to Himself through the death of Christ in His physical body. As a result, He has brought you into His own presence, and you are holy and blameless as you stand before Him without a single fault.'* NLT

So, with this in mind where does that leave the Law of God today? In the Old Testament the Law was enshrined within the confines of the Mosaic Administration. We know that this administration is no longer required, as Jesus fulfilled all the duties of the priests. However, Jesus didn't come to do away with the Law of God. The Law is eternal, but the Mosaic administration which housed the Law was temporal. So, what becomes of this Law in the New Testament? Well previously the Law was written upon stone tablets, external to man. Now it is internal and written on our hearts and minds: Hebrews 10:16 *'"This is the new covenant I will make with my people on that day, says the LORD: I will put my laws in their hearts, and I will write them on their minds."'* NLT

The Law in the New Testament is no longer housed in the Mosaic administration. Now the Law is enshrined where it always should be - in the Melchizedek administration. We have moved from the Priesthood of Aaron to the Priesthood of Melchizedek. This simple fact has caused much confusion, especially for those who try to observe the Law of Moses. Yes, the Law is eternal but now it is enshrined within new promises in a far superior covenant. The Law is now housed in the priesthood of Melchizedek. This is a huge subject which is really a book in its own right, but this should give you enough to go on with! I highly recommend reading the book of Hebrews over and over again to understand this teaching.

Probably one of the most shocking statements in the book of Hebrews is found in Hebrews 13:10 *'We have an altar from which the priests in the Tabernacle have no right to eat.'* NLT. We come before the altar which is in heaven. The heavenly pattern is the Melchizedek priesthood, not the priesthood of Aaron. Therefore, those under the Mosaic Administration have no right to eat from the heavenly altar, only those who have now entered the New Covenant through the blood of Jesus. The Administration of Moses was only a shadow and type of the reality based in heaven. We no longer serve in the Tabernacle of Moses. Now we serve the True Tabernacle in heaven and minister as priests under the order of Melchizedek, which the following scriptures make clear:

Hebrews 8:5 *'They serve a copy and shadow of the heavenly things. For when Moses was about to erect the tent, he was instructed by God, saying, "See that you make everything according to the pattern that was shown you on the mountain."'* ESV

Hebrews 10:1 *'The law is only a shadow of the good things that are coming--not the realities themselves. For this reason it can never, by the same sacrifices repeated endlessly year after year, make perfect those who draw near to worship.'* NIV

Revelation 15:5 *'Then I looked and saw that the Temple in heaven, God's Tabernacle, was thrown wide open.'* NLT

Revelation 5:10 *'You have made them to be a kingdom and priests to serve our God, and they will reign on the earth."'* NIV

So, what has all this got to do with tithing? Well under the Mosaic administration, tithing was exacted from the people. They had no choice. It just had to be paid. This money was then used to pay the priests, upkeep the tabernacle/temple and help the poor. However, in the order of Melchizedek tithing is not exacted. Rather it is expected to be given willingly, lovingly and most importantly, given in faith.

Now there are many who say tithing is not under the New Covenant and there is very little written about it in the New Testament. The simple fact is tithing was practised before the Law and not just after the Law.

A verse which pops up in respect to New Testament giving is found in 2 Corinthians 9:7: *'Each of you should give what you have decided in your heart to give, not reluctantly or under compulsion, for God loves a cheerful giver.'* NIV

The context of this passage is to do with a large offering being collected for other churches in need of financial help. We see here a clear distinction between *'tithes and offerings'*, (Malachi 3:8). Tithes are our basic act of worship to God, and offerings are over and above the tithe. In other words, we do both not just one or the other. Tithing is a part of our worship each week or month to our Great High Priest

Jesus (Melchizedek. See Hebrews 5:10 & 6:20). Our offerings are additional gifts we give as the situation requires or as the Spirit leads.

Hebrews 7:4-6   *'Now observe how great this man [Melchizedek - Jesus] was to whom Abraham, the patriarch, gave a tenth of the choicest spoils. And those indeed of the sons of Levi who receive the priest's office have commandment in the Law to collect a tenth from the people, that is, from their brethren, although these are descended from Abraham. But the one whose genealogy is not traced from them collected a tenth from Abraham and blessed the one who had the promises.'* NASB

This verse show us that Abraham gladly gave a tithe and Melchizedek gladly received it. So, tithing is not so much an Old or New Testament concept, rather it is a biblical one which spans the beginning of the Bible to the end. In the New Covenant under the priesthood of Melchizedek it is offered freely with love, reverence and most importantly faith.

CHAPTER TWENTY ONE

TIME FOR A NEW NAME

Genesis 17:5 *"No longer shall your name be Abram, but your name shall be Abraham; for I have made you the father of a multitude of nations".* NASB

By a simple name change, God prophesied the destiny of Abram (exalted father) to become Abraham (father of many nations). We then have the wonderful moment when God also changed the name of Sarai (my princess) to Sarah (princess).

Genesis 17:15-16 *'Then God said to Abraham, "As for Sarai your wife, you shall not call her name Sarai, but Sarah shall be her name. I will bless her, and indeed I will give you a son by her. Then I will bless her, and she shall be a mother of nations; kings of peoples will come from her."'* NASB

We could ask, why the name was changed because Sarai and Sarah almost mean the same thing. Well, to Abraham, his wife was already his princess, but now, in God's timing, she was given the actual royal title of 'Princess'. Why? Because now God was about to heal Sarah's womb and so fulfil His promise to Abraham that from his seed would come the Messiah.

From this moment on Abraham is "the father of many nations" and Sarah is the "princess of nations" even though, as yet, nothing had changed. Every time they spoke out their new names, they were confessing the word of God and so co-working with His Holy Spirit. Faith comes by hearing, and Abraham was now able to 'see' the promise being *called into existence* and that it would be fulfilled through Sarah in some miraculous way.

Romans 4:17 *'As it is written, "I have made you (Abraham) the father of many nations"—in the presence of the God in whom he believed, who gives life to the dead **and calls into existence the things that do not exist**.'* ESV

The Prophetic promise realised through faith...

The reality that *faith comes by hearing,* has to do with the creative power of the word of God in the mouth of the believer.

Hebrews 4:12 *'For the word of God is living and active and sharper than any two-edged sword, and piercing as far as the division of soul and spirit, of both joints and marrow, and able to judge the thoughts and intentions of the heart.'* NASB

Prophecy, if from God, is actually living and active. For all words from God are alive. They have the ability to come to pass, through the Holy Spirit, who *watches over God's word to perform it* (Jeremiah 1:12). If we look at Genesis 1:3, we can see the creative power of the word in action, spoken by God and performed by the Holy Spirit.

Genesis 1:3 *'Then God said, "Let there be light"; and there was light.'* NASB

In this next verse we are told that the universe was made by faith.

Hebrews 11:3 *'**By faith** we understand that **the worlds were prepared by the word of God**, so that what is seen was not made out of things which are visible.'* NASB

In the beginning, God literally called into being that which did not exist. God used His faith and 'spoke the word', the Holy Spirit empowered the word and the job was done. This kind of speaking is known as decreeing and proclaiming. As believers we too can do this by speaking to the mountains in our lives and telling mountains to move. Speaking to our mountains in life is not just a faith thing. It is also a prophetic thing. Prophecy is calling forth that which is not into existence. There are characters throughout the bible who were told to speak and call forth a reality that was not yet realised in the natural realm. For example, Ezekiel was told to prophecy to the mountains of Israel (Ezekiel 6:1-7).

Prophecy and faith are interlinked. Prophecy reveals and calls forth the will of God, whereas faith comes from hearing the prophetic word and becomes the substance of that spoken word. Remember, faith is the substance of things not yet seen. In time, the prophetic/spoken word will manifest as reality. This is all revealed and borne out in the life of Abraham.

To deeper understand the nature of prophecy and faith we need to return to Romans 4:13-24 *'It was not through the law that Abraham and his offspring received the promise that he would be heir of the world, but through the righteousness that comes by faith. For if those who depend on the law are heirs, faith means nothing and the promise is worthless, because the law brings wrath. And where there is no law there is no transgression. Therefore, the promise comes by faith, so that it may be by grace and may be guaranteed to all Abraham's offspring--not only to those who are of the law but also to those who have the faith of Abraham. He is the father of us all. As it is written: "I have made you a father of many nations." He is our father in the sight of God, in whom he believed--the God who gives life to the dead and calls into being things that were not. Against all hope, Abraham in hope believed and so became the father of many nations, just as it had been said to him, "So shall your offspring be." Without weakening in his faith, he faced the fact that his body was as good as dead--since he was about a hundred years old--and that Sarah's womb was also dead. Yet he did not waver through unbelief regarding the promise of God, but was strengthened in his faith and gave glory to God, being fully persuaded that God had power to do what he had promised. This is why "it was credited to him as righteousness." The words "it was credited to him" were written not for him alone, but also for us, to whom God will credit righteousness-*

-for us who believe in him who raised Jesus our Lord from the dead.' NIV

Let's work through this section verse by verse. I will paraphrase sections to help highlight the point.

V13 *'It was not through the law that Abraham and his offspring received the promise that he would be heir of the world, but through the righteousness that comes by faith.'*

The prophetic promise to Abraham concerning his becoming the father of many nations was received **through faith** not works or efforts of the flesh.

V16 *'Therefore, the promise comes by faith, so that it may be by grace and may be guaranteed to all Abraham's offspring--not only to those who are of the law but also to those who have the faith of Abraham. He is the father of us all.'*

This verse is very important. The promise is received by faith through grace. It can be anything from God's word such as salvation, healing, provision etc. Whatever the promise, it is always received by grace through faith (See Ephesians 2:8).

V17 *'As it is written: "I have made you a father of many nations." He is our father in the sight of God, in whom he believed--the God who gives life to the dead and calls into being things that were not.'*

God gives the 'Word' and the 'Prophecy'. *"I have appointed you the father of many nations..."* This is the word which Abraham heard and believed upon by faith. Remember, God calls into being those things that are not as though they are. **This is the prophetic and faith power of the word of God!** Once the prophetic is released and discharged, faith takes hold of it to see it become a reality.

V18 *'Against all hope, Abraham in hope believed and so became the father of many nations, just as it had been said to him, "So shall your offspring be."'*

'Hope against all hope...' i.e. when the situation was out of the realm of human possibility, Abraham still believed by faith. and thus eventually became the father of many nations **according to what God had said.**

V19 *'Without weakening in his faith, he faced the fact that his body was as good as dead--since he was about a hundred years old--and that Sarah's womb was also dead.'*

Looking at his own weak and pathetic body, Abraham considered it irrelevant because of his faith in God.

V20 *'Yet he did not waver through unbelief regarding the promise of God, but was strengthened in his faith and gave glory to God,'*

Because of God's word which he trusted above all things, he did not waver in unbelief. But was strengthened in faith. How? By giving glory to God that the promise would surely happen.

Abraham had learned a key principle: Continually praise and thank God for the reality of His promises!

V21 *'being fully persuaded that God had power to do what he had promised.'*

Here is another key. Abraham became utterly convinced God would do what He said He would do. How? Because he meditated upon the promise and from v20 kept praising God for it. Thus, faith became the substance of the hope which came

through the creative prophetic word of God. It then became a reality by the power of the Holy Spirit. Why? How?

Jeremiah 1:12 *'… I (God) watch over My word to perform it…'*

God always watches over His word to perform and activate it. It is the power of the Holy Spirit that does this.

So now that you understand some basic theory on how this stuff works, maybe it is time for you to start confessing the word of God for yourself! Give the Holy Spirit something to work with! Don't go around speaking negative confessions all day long. Change your language and start loading your mouth with the word of God. The Holy Spirit will only watch over "God's word". Remember, the word of God is living and active. Once you begin speaking His word out, it will immediately start to work. But it can take time, so do not be discouraged if you do not see instant results. Remember the word is the seed. Mark 4:26-29 *'He also said, "This is what the kingdom of God is like. A man scatters seed on the ground. Night and day, whether he sleeps or gets up, the seed sprouts and grows, though he does not know how. All by itself the soil produces grain--first the stalk, then the head, then the full kernel in the head. As soon as the grain is ripe, he puts the sickle to it, because the harvest has come."*

CHAPTER TWENTY TWO

THE MULTIPLICATION PRINCIPLE

Genesis 22:17-18
'That in blessing I will bless thee, and in multiplying I will multiply thy seed as the stars of the heaven, and as the sand which is upon the sea shore; and thy seed shall possess the gate of his enemies; And in thy seed shall all the nations of the earth be blessed; because thou hast obeyed my voice.'
KJV

This passage of scripture is another confirmation and ratification of the Abrahamic covenant. It seems, God enjoys taking every opportunity to bless Abraham and his seed! This passage should excite us today, because this blessing is as much for us now as it was for Abraham. It is a prophetic declaration over all the seed of Abraham by God Himself. We are a blessed people because God has chosen to bless us. We are indeed blessed by the Blessed One.

When the world looks at us they should see that we are blessed of God. It doesn't matter if you are flipping burgers for a living or writing and composing music for the latest major movie. If you are blessed of God, then you are blessed. So, we, as believers need to simply do just that, believe! We need to get it into our consciousness that we are blessed. You might look at your circumstances and situations in your life and think that you don't look or feel blessed, but that is actually irrelevant. God's truth trumps your circumstances. For God's word is Spirit and Truth and it is eternal (John 6:63). Regardless how difficult our lives may be, they are merely transitory in comparison to the word of God. The quicker we understand and believe in faith that we are blessed by God, the quicker that blessing can get to work in us and through us.

'That in blessing I will bless thee'... We should take note, that this is God speaking, the creator of all the earth, the universe, and all the heavenly realms and He has chosen to bless

us. Wow! If God is for us who can be against us? (Romans 8:31). You may think that you are not worthy to be blessed in such a way. Well, praise God, because in truth, no one is worthy of such a blessing. It is simply the grace of God and we just have to live with the fact that He has chosen to bless us. As we saw in previous chapters the whole point of this blessing is that we are blessed to be a blessing and sow into peoples lives the very kingdom of God. The sower will always reap from what he has sown, that is why Jesus says it is more blessed to give than to receive (Acts 20:35). If we are on the giving end of the blessing then we will always be on the receiving end. We will always reap what we sow, remember though, the heart attitude is to stay on the giving end of the blessing, in an attitude of love. There is no place for self-service and self-interest in the kingdom of God!

'That in blessing I will bless thee, and in multiplying I will multiply...'

This passage shows us an exciting aspect of God's blessing: Multiplication! To paraphrase this text into the first person we have *'In being blessed of God I bless, in the multiplication of that blessing I multiply.'* Some may think I am stretching the text here, but let's look at how Jesus used the blessing to multiply.

Luke 9:16 *'Then He took the five loaves and the two fish, and looking up to heaven,* **He blessed them***, and broke them,* **and kept giving them** *to the disciples to set before the people'* NASB. This passage from Luke's gospel, is the well-known account of Jesus feeding over 5000 people with five loaves and two fishes. What I want the reader to understand here, is that although this was a wonderful miracle, Jesus was actually operating under the same Abrahamic blessing you and I are under. He blessed the loaves and fishes and they multiplied. Jesus understood the Abrahamic blessing as He was the very One who had given it to Abraham! He merely operated in it by faith!

There may be some reading this who are thinking that I am now diminishing the power of Jesus' miracles. Absolutely not! The point I am trying to make here is that Jesus did not come to earth to show off that He is God. Although fully God, He also came into this world fully human, with a mission to identify with humanity. He came to show the way for every believer, He was the perfect Master who we can imitate and follow as His disciples. Jesus made this very clear in the gospels as well as encouraging us to do likewise.

Luke 6:40 'A disciple is not above his teacher, but everyone who is perfectly trained **will be like** his teacher.' NKJV

Matthew 28:18-20 'Then Jesus came and spoke to them, saying, "All authority has been given to Me in heaven and on earth. "**Go therefore and make disciples** of all the nations, baptising them in the name of the Father and of the Son and of the Holy Spirit, "teaching them to observe **all things that I have commanded you**; and lo, I am with you always, even to the end of the age." Amen.' NKJV

John 14:12 "Most assuredly, I say to you, he who believes in Me, **the works that I do he will do also**; and greater works than these he will do, because I go to My Father.' NKJV

Spiritual Authority

Verse 17: '...and thy seed shall possess the gate of his enemies...'

There are two contexts to the 'seed' I am writing about in this chapter. Firstly, the primary meaning is referring to 'The Seed' which is Jesus (See Chapter 6). The secondary context is written for us and about us. We are the seed of Abraham and we shall possess the gate of our enemies.

Galatians 3:29 *'And if you belong to Christ, then you are Abraham's seed, heirs according to the promise.'* HCSB

Galatians makes it very clear. We are the seed of Abraham, thus we also possess the gates of our enemies. Why? Because Genesis 22:17 tells us that we will! Some may see this as a conflict of interests. Surely, we are to love our enemies not be victorious over them? This is true, but the New Testament makes it very clear according to Ephesians 6:12 that there is another level: *'For we wrestle not against flesh and blood, but against principalities, against powers, against the rulers of the darkness of this world, against spiritual wickedness in high places.'* KJV

We have all, at times, experienced the enemy possessing the gates of our lives rather than the other way around. The problem with the Christian walk is that we often come against hardships because of our lack of understanding of the bible: Hosea 4:6 *'My people are destroyed for lack of knowledge…'* KJV

It is simply a lack of knowledge, that makes us vulnerable and can give the enemy a foothold in our lives. When we understand that we have authority over the devil and that he has no legal right to the 'gates' of our lives, things start to change. So, in the areas of spiritual warfare, we should be on the offensive, fighting for our marriages, families, health, finances, churches etc. These are the 'gates' the enemy targets in our lives. But the Abrahamic blessing takes it a step further. Not only do we have victory over the enemy, but we also have the right to take hold and possess his gates. This is because Jesus bound the 'strong man' for us on The Cross, so we now have the right to plunder the enemies camp!

Mark 3:27 *'Let me illustrate this further. Who is powerful enough to enter the house of a strong man like Satan and plunder his goods? Only someone even stronger--someone who could tie him up and then plunder his house.'* NLT

All the enemies 'goods' are stolen. Stolen from God and stolen from man. Satan tricked and stole authority from Adam in the garden of Eden. Satan through manipulation and lies robs mankind of joy, peace and love. When we recognise that satan is a thief, a destroyer, a prowler, we should get aggressive, by standing firm and holding our ground, and by becoming pro-active and praying against his strategies in the lives of others.

The Abrahamic blessing is emphatic. We will possess the gates of our enemies. We have to walk in it and take it up by faith. We need to take the time to ponder and meditate on these things until they so fill our inner man that they change how we think and act. It's one thing to know you have authority in Christ, but it's a whole different reality to actually walk in that authority.

CHAPTER TWENTY THREE

BLESSING DURING FAMINE

Genesis 26:1 & 12-14 *'Now there was a famine in the land, besides the previous famine that had occurred in the days of Abraham. So, Isaac went to Gerar, to Abimelech king of the Philistines... Now Isaac sowed in that land and reaped in the same year a hundredfold. And the LORD blessed him, and the man became rich, and continued to grow richer until he became very wealthy;   for he had possessions of flocks and herds and a great household, so that the Philistines envied him.'* NASB

These verses are remarkable. We see a miraculous example of the Abrahamic blessing in Isaac's life, occurring during a time of great famine, when the natural world around him ceased to function.

Britain as a nation has gone through a long period of sustained prosperity, but I believe that there is a coming day when our natural world will also cease to function, as the financial systems fail and collapse.

Hebrews 12:27-28 teaches us that everything that can be shaken will be shaken. However, we the Church, are of a kingdom that cannot be shaken. In that hour, we will have to be operating in a dimension of faith and understanding at a much higher level than we are right now. We may have to trust God for the miraculous in our daily lives, as we continue living out kingdom principles of sowing and reaping to cope with the demands that will come upon us.

In the days ahead there will need to be a clear separation between the church and the world. As in Moses' day, while Egypt was being struck by all manner of sorrows, the Hebrews in the land of Goshen were separated and thus not effected.

So, extreme troubles call for extreme grace, and I believe in the days ahead the church will be given a special dispensation to move in a miraculous flow of grace and faith, the likes of which this world has rarely seen. Days of miraculous multiplication will take place before our very eyes. Just as Jesus multiplied the loaves and fishes, He will do so again through the church in wonderful ways, to help us cope with the demands of the desperate needs around us.

Psalm 37:19 *'They will not be ashamed in the time of evil, And in the days of famine they will have abundance..'* NASB

Job 5:20-22 states that we shall laugh at the days of famine. However, we must start preparing for the unthinkable now, by ploughing the ground, using the principles of sowing and reaping and living on the pathway of faith. We need to become competent 'kingdom farmers' right now! So that when the famine comes, we will be able to keep sowing and reaping even when the world's systems of prosperity fail and may even be broken beyond repair.

So we must 'know that we know' our source of provision is God, not the local bank or the international stock markets. It is time right now to stop playing with the world's systems of prosperity and instead start tapping into God's systems via sowing and reaping. In the days ahead God will prosper His church, if we apply and abide by His kingdom principles. Not for our own ends and selfish pleasures, but for the advancement of the kingdom of God to meet the needs of a needy world through the hope of the gospel.

The world has been hit many times by sudden famines and intense poverty: Acts 11:28 *'And one of them named Agabus stood up and foretold by the Spirit that there would be a great famine over all the world (this took place in the days of Claudius)'* ESV

This famine was very severe, so much so, that it was recorded in Roman history. Many of the churches were in need of assistance. We read in 2 Corinthians chapters 8 and 9 about a large offering collected from the Corinthian church and then distributed to those in need. Many churches needed financial support to feed and clothe people for indefinite periods of time. So, these offerings were not meagre donations. We are talking vast sums of money! They were half-yearly, and according to 2 Corinthians 9:2 the Corinthian church was given a year to prepare to give. With this in mind let's take a closer look at 2 Corinthians 9:6-14. Remember the context of this whole chapter and the preceding one is financial provision.

2 Corinthians 9:6 *'Now this I say, he who sows sparingly will also reap sparingly, and he who sows bountifully will also reap bountifully.'* NASB

We need to remember that when we sow into the Kingdom of God, we do not just receive back what was sown, we always get a greater return.

Mark 4:8 *'And other seeds fell into good soil and produced grain, growing up and increasing and yielding thirtyfold and sixtyfold and a hundredfold.'"* ESV

This passage teaches that every seed sown on GOOD GROUND has the potential to multiply 40, 60, 100 times more. This is a key kingdom principle. Every seed sown has the maximum potential of a hundredfold return. To be fair, a hundred fold return is rare but is a sign of great grace and favour. Any return on sowing in the kingdom is a supernatural blessing. I believe in the days ahead we will see larger returns and even hundredfold returns, because the need for such a grace will be highly evident. If the need is great and the church is doing things correctly, then God will supply all our needs according to His riches in glory (Philippians 4:19).

We previously looked at Isaac in Genesis 26:12 and how he received a hundredfold return in a time of famine. But do you want to know what was so notable about that miracle? In verse 1 of chapter 26 it says that because the famine was so severe, Isaac dwelt in Gerar with the Philistines. So God literally blessed Isaac right in front of his future enemies.

Psalm 23:5 *'You prepare a table before me in the presence of my enemies. You anoint my head with oil; my cup overflows.'* NIV

Another obvious example of how God provides for His people during times of famine, is the story of Joseph and how God had sent him as a boy to Egypt to became a mighty political ruler. Why? To save Israel, God's people, from one of the worst famines in history.

We saw earlier how Agabus the prophet in the New Testament warned of the coming famine, and how the church prepared and dealt with it accordingly (Acts 11:28). We see through these bible stories a God who is interested in His people not only as a people group, but also as individuals.

In 1 Kings 17 we have the prophet Elijah being provided for during a time of harsh famine. God used ravens and even an angel to provide food for him. Again in 1 Kings 17:8-16 we have the story of Elijah and the widow of Zerephath. This poor widow was already to cook a last meal for herself and her son, then prepare to die of starvation. A terrible and ghastly prospect for anyone. Then the prophet Elijah came to meet her according to the word of the Lord. He then gave her a prophetic blessing by saying, *'Make me some food and give me a bite to eat first and then God will bless you, and your food supply will not run out till the famine be ended.'*

Most people would have told Elijah to 'get lost' but this widow heard the word of the Lord, obeyed the word of God and received a miracle (a prophet's reward,) which saved her and her son from certain death.

This is how the church and the world around us will survive in the days of financial famine ahead. **Hear the word of the Lord and do the word of the Lord.** God cares for His own but He also has compassion on the ungodly. Through Joseph Egypt was saved. Through Elijah a gentile widow and her son were saved.

Matthew 5:45 *'...He (God) causes his sun to rise on the evil and the good, and sends rain on the righteous and the unrighteous.'* NIV

In the days ahead, God will want His church, which is His body, to thrive and prosper during the days of famine. This is not just for her own sake, but to be a light to the gentiles and to be a blessing to save spiritual Egypt from utter ruin. For God will take great pity on the unsaved in that hour.

2 Peter 3:9 *'The Lord is not slow in keeping His promise, as some understand slowness. Instead He is patient with You, not wanting anyone to perish, but everyone to come to repentance.'* NIV

Isaiah 60:1-3 *'Arise, shine, for your light has come, and the glory of the LORD has risen upon you. For behold, darkness shall cover the earth, and thick darkness the peoples; but the LORD will arise upon you, and His glory will be seen upon you. And nations shall come to your light, and kings to the brightness of your rising.'* NIV

In Acts 4:32-35 we see a church moving in such generosity there was NO ONE who lacked anything: *'All the believers were united in heart and mind. And they felt that what they owned was not their own, so they shared everything they had. The apostles testified powerfully to the resurrection of the Lord Jesus, and **God's great blessing was upon them <u>all</u>**. **There were no needy people among them**, because those who owned land or houses would sell them.'* NLT. This generosity was happening during a time of revival. Signs and wonders and miracles were being performed. Many people were getting saved and healed, and families ravaged by poverty were provided for. This is a revival culture in action, as God's heart is always for His people to be looked after body, spirit and soul.

We see in Matthew 14:14 how Jesus had compassion and healed the sick. He also performed a miracle for many who were tired and hungry, multiplying the loaves and fishes, so they were all well fed with plenty left over.

Our God is a God of loving kindness and tender mercies. Some Christians need to get off their self-righteous soap boxes and stop spewing hatred and anger at the world and even their own brothers and sisters. It is God who judges the unrighteous, not us. Our job is to show gentleness, compassion and love to one another and to a dying, needy world that have rejected God because the devil has blinded them.

God hates it when a lost soul slips into hell. It is not God's will that any should perish. So, church arise! We are the Body of Christ on the earth, and in this late hour, Oh how we need to *'return to our first love'*! Recapture the compassion of God for the lost! and reveal Jesus' heart as we preach, share, and intercede for a great harvest in these last days.

CHAPTER TWENTY FOUR

THE BLESSING CONTINUED

Genesis 27:28-29 *'Now may God give you of the dew of heaven, and of the fatness of the earth, and an abundance of grain and new wine; May peoples serve you, and nations bow down to you; be master of your brothers, and may your mother's sons bow down to you. Cursed be those who curse you, and blessed be those who bless you."* NASB

The first thing we need to see here is that God is our source. The "heavens" and "the fatness of the earth" only yield blessings to us because God has cut covenant with us. God alone is our source. God is <u>The Source</u>. It is His command which opens and closes the heavens.
Never make the mistake of thinking that spiritual blessings are not physical ones, and that physical ones are not spiritual. God wants to give us glimpses and experiences of the heavenly realm even while we are here upon the earth. A clear example of this is the manna which came down from heaven to provide for the children of Israel during the 40 years in the wilderness. They had no idea that they were eating and being sustained by the Messiah Jesus, Who is the Bread of Heaven (See John 6:47-51). This manna was a physical manifestation of a heavenly, spiritual reality. Jesus, The Word, is The Bread of Life. *'Man cannot live just by bread alone but by every Word that proceeds out of the mouth of God'* (Matthew 4:4).

Heaven and earth are intrinsically bound together for the Christian. However, due to a Greek mindset, we tend to separate out the physical from the spiritual. The carnal world around us does everything it can to disconnect itself from the heavenly pattern, by changing laws of the land and living in rebellion to the law of God and His kingdom. We should not make the same error. First the natural then the spiritual (1Corinthians 15:46).

In the Lord's prayer we are told to pray for God's will and kingdom to come down here upon the earth, as it is already being done in heaven (Matthew 6:9-10). We can also make errors in our understanding by thinking our day to day secular work is somehow not spiritual. This is not the case! You and I are carriers of the kingdom of heaven. Like yeast spreading in the dough, we are to infect and affect those around us with the life, law and power of the kingdom of God. We really do matter and make a difference as believers. If ten righteous people had lived in Sodom and Gomorrah it would not have been destroyed (Genesis 18:32). You and I can always, and in every situation, make the difference of life and death, blessing or judgement.

Acts 13:47 *"For so the Lord has commanded us, 'I HAVE PLACED YOU AS A LIGHT FOR THE GENTILES, THAT YOU MAY BRING SALVATION TO THE END OF THE EARTH.'"* NASB

Genesis 27:28 *'Now may God give you of the dew of heaven, and of the fatness of the earth, and an abundance of grain and new wine;'*
In this verse, God is not referring to the dew on the grass in the morning, He is speaking of His heavenly blessings of provision and refreshment.

Many of us are happy to receive God's abundant spiritual blessings, yet part of the Abrahamic blessing is to be blessed in the natural too. This is where all manner of issues become apparent. To accept that God wants to bless His people with the fatness of the earth is a real stumbling block to some. It is like the principle of healing. Does God really want to heal all people like Jesus did when He walked the earth? Does God want to prosper His people like He did Abraham, Isaac, Jacob, Joseph, David, Solomon etc.? God does not want anyone to be in a place of financial lack. Constant poverty is under the curse of the law, remember our key scripture (Galatians 3: 13-14) we have now been redeemed from the curse of the law.

The bible teaches us that we have been redeemed from the curse of the law, but it doesn't say anywhere that we have been redeemed from The Blessing of the law. Yet this is the mindset of many. We have been redeemed from the curse, not The Blessing.

There is also an eschatological aspect to The Blessing as well, for Matthew 5:5 says *'Blessed are the meek, for they shall inherit the earth.'*, and *so w*hen Jesus returns we will rule and reign with Him upon the earth.

2 Timothy 2:12 *'If we endure, we will also reign with him; if we deny him, he also will deny us;'* ESV

Revelation 5:10 *'and you have made them a kingdom and priests to our God, and they shall reign on the earth."* ESV

Revelation 20:6 *'Blessed and holy is the one who shares in the first resurrection! Over such the second death has no power, but they will be priests of God and of Christ, and they will reign with him for a thousand years.'* ESV

It is clear that the fulness of the Abrahamic blessing will finally manifest when Jesus returns. However, we can have that kingdom manifest here and now if we pray for it and take it by faith. Remember this is what Jesus tells us to pray in the *Lord's Prayer.*

Matthew 6:10 *'May your kingdom come, may your will be done on the earth as it is in heaven.'*

So, yes, we can have the Abrahamic covenant operating in our lives, however there can be a cost attached as we see in Mark 10:30 *'who will not receive a hundredfold **now in this time**, houses and brothers and sisters and mothers and children and lands, **with persecutions**, and in the age to come eternal life.'* ESV

Why does this passage say that we would be blessed but with persecutions? This is because the blessing of the Lord is supernatural and highly offensive to some. It can also make people jealous and critical. Remember Isaac, who experienced serious prosperity from God in a time of great lack, and then look at the consequences of his harvest and the reaction of the surrounding people.

Genesis 26:12-14 *'Now Isaac sowed in that land and reaped in the same year a hundredfold. And the LORD blessed him, and the man **became rich**, and **continued to grow richer** until he became **very wealthy**; for he had possessions of flocks and herds and a great household, <u>**so that the Philistines envied him.**</u>'* NASB

The carnal mind staggers at the power and the goodness of God, but it is those who 'stagger not' who receive God's covenantal benefits by grace, through faith. Look at Abraham as an example:

Romans 4:20-21 *'Yet, with respect to the promise of God, he did not waver in unbelief but grew strong in faith, giving glory to God and being fully assured that what God had promised, He was able also to perform.'* NASB

Romans 4:16 *'So the promise is received by faith. It is given as a free gift. And we are all certain to receive it, whether or not we live according to the law of Moses, if we have faith like Abraham's. For Abraham is the father of all who believe.'* NLT

God wants to bless us with the fatness of the earth. Why? So that in blessing He will establish His covenant upon the earth.

Deuteronomy 8:18 *'But you shall remember the LORD your God, for it is He who is giving you power to make wealth, that He may confirm His covenant which He swore to your fathers, as it is this day.'* NASB

So God, by giving us the ability and power to prosper actually confirms and affirms the covenant He made with Abraham. God wants to bless us with prosperity. Now for those still concerned with this reality, I need to reiterate that the word in the Hebrew bible translated as prosperity comes from the Hebrew word *'Shalom.'* This is an all-encompassing word which is rich in meaning. It denotes wholeness, health, vitality, peace, secureness, and prosperity. To have God's covenantal *'Shalom'* means God has everything covered and you can rest in the peace of that truth.

Psalm 35:27 *'Let them shout for joy and rejoice, who favour my vindication; And let them say continually, "The LORD be magnified, **Who delights in the prosperity of His servant**."'*

Proverbs 10:22 *'The blessing of the LORD makes rich, and he adds no sorrow with it.'* ESV

2 Corinthians 9:8 *'And God will generously provide all you need. Then you will always have everything you need and plenty left over to share with others.'* NLT

Deuteronomy 28:11-12 *'And the LORD will make you abound in prosperity, in the fruit of your womb and in the fruit of your livestock and in the fruit of your ground, within the land that the LORD swore to your fathers to give you. The LORD will open to you his good treasury, the heavens, to give the rain to your land in its season and to bless all the work of your hands. And you shall lend to many nations, but you shall not borrow.'* ESV

Now, here is a hypothetical question for you: How many scriptures need to be quoted before we really start to believe that God wants to bless and prosper us? Jesus came that we might have **life** and have it **in abundance**: John 10:10 *'The thief comes only to steal and kill and destroy. I came that they may have life and have it abundantly.'* ESV

To be in a place of lack financially is a part of the curse of the law from which we have now been redeemed. The blessing of Abraham belongs to all who believe in Jesus.

Galatians 3:29 *'And if you are Christ's, then you are Abraham's offspring, heirs according to promise.'* ESV

When we understand that Jesus embodied the curse of the law on the cross, we begin to understand other scriptures, such as 2 Corinthians 8:9 *'For you know the grace of our Lord Jesus Christ, that though He was rich, yet for your sake He became poor, so that you through His poverty might become rich'* NASB

This scripture is enormous in its scope, as it is dealing with how Jesus, who is 'very God', made Himself poor by stripping Himself of all His glory and taking upon Himself human flesh. He did this so that through His poverty and being stripped naked upon the cross, He would make us heirs with Him and rich like Him. Rich in salvation and co-heirs of all God owns.

When Jesus went to the cross He became sin, sickness and poverty. He became the embodiment of the curse of the law, so that we could be made whole and full of the blessings of Abraham. Remember, these blessings are both physical and spiritual, they go hand in hand, as the blessing always starts in our inner man.

2 John 3:2 *'Beloved, I pray that in all respects you may prosper and be in good health, **just as your soul prospers**.'* NASB

2 Peter 1:3-4 *'Seeing that His divine power has granted to us everything pertaining to life and godliness, through the true knowledge of Him who called us by His own glory and excellence. For by these He has granted to us His precious and magnificent promises, so that by them you may become partakers of the divine nature, having escaped the corruption that is in the world by lust.'* NASB

CONCLUSIONS

Genesis 28:3-4 *"May God Almighty **bless you** and make you **fruitful** and **multiply** you, that you may become a company of peoples. May He also give you <u>**the blessing of Abraham**</u>, to you <u>**and to your descendants**</u> with you, **that you may possess the land** of your sojournings, which God gave to Abraham."*

The purpose of this book has been to highlight several key themes concerning the blessing of Abraham, and how important it is for us today. When our 'eyes' are open to its reality, we will see it interwoven all through the bible.

So, to recap, let us take to heart the truth, that when we accept Jesus into our lives, we not only receive our eternal salvation, but we are placed in covenant with God and can legally enter into The Blessing of Abraham. When all was lost at the fall, God in His wonderful mercy and grace set into motion a plan to bring man back into relationship with Himself, back into the blessing and back into paradise. This is the gospel!

The Cross enables us to enter the covenant of Abraham, it releases the blessing and ultimately leads us back to paradise when we go to glory, or when Jesus returns, whichever comes first. So, when we understand that we are saved to a full and wonderful gospel/covenant with God, and that He wants to restore our lives into a place mirroring the kingdom of heaven, then the sky is the limit. Jesus came preaching a full gospel, teaching us how to *live life and have it in abundance* (John 10:10). We know that not one single human deserves this blessing, but God chooses to lavish His love, care and blessings upon us anyway. The reason why we even love God in the first place is because He first loved us. Our God is a wonderful and beautiful God! Who can be compared to Him?

Finally, be encouraged! It is the blessing of Abraham that will enable *you* to enter into your promised land. It will empower *you* to move into the calling that God has placed upon your life. Remember 'The Blessing' is God's covenantal favour towards *you*. This means the Holy Spirit will be watching over God's word to perform it for *you* (Jeremiah 1:12). It means that angels will be ministering to *you* (Hebrews 1:14). It means that all of heaven is backing *you*. There are no limits to God's blessing, so our response is to simply believe it and walk in it. Of course, there will be trials and testings on the journey, but if God is for you who can ultimately be against you? No one! God is good, praise His name!

God bless you all

Pastor Chris Wickland

BOOKS BY CHRISTOPHER WICKLAND

Faith School (Learning to walk by faith the easy way)
The Biblical Importance of Israel and everything else that goes with it
The Blessing of Abraham

CONTACT THE AUTHOR

If you wish to contact the author of this work please feel free to email this address.

livingwordchurches@yahoo.co.uk

www.livingwordchurchnetwork.uk

A PRAYER FOR SALVATION

If you feel after reading this book, that you would like to know Jesus as your Lord and Saviour, please simply pray this prayer of salvation.

Dear Lord Jesus. Come into my life and be my Lord, my God and my friend.
Forgive me for all my sins, wash me clean, change me and set me free.
Let me never be the same again.
Jesus I believe You died for me. Thank you that you rose from the dead, and now pray for me from heaven.
Help me to live for you, to become a disciple and fulfil everything You have called me to do.
I thank you that I am now forgiven and a child of God.
In Jesus Name. Amen

To grow in your new life as a Christian you need to follow a simple plan...

Get yourself into a good local church. Make new friends and grow in your faith with others.

Read your bible daily. This will be a form of spiritual food to help you grow in your new faith. It's recommend that you start with the gospel of Mark.

You are now in a relationship with The Living God. Like any relationship you need to talk. Start talking (praying) to God today.